DINING SECRETS™
of Indiana
9TH EDITION

CONTENTS

150 Indiana Cities & Towns
featuring unique restaurants, interesting places to visit, and special treats to enjoy!

Alexandria	Edinburgh	Lafayette	Remington
Anderson	Elkhart	LaPorte	Richmond
Angola	Ellettsville	Lawrenceburg	Roanoke
Atlanta	Elwood	Leavenworth	Rochester
Auburn	Eugene	Lebanon	Rosedale
Avilla	Evansville	Lincoln City	Salem
Avon	Fairmount	LIzton	Sellersburg
Batesville	Fair Oaks	Logansport	Seymour
Battle Ground	Farmland	Madison	Schererville
Bedford	Ferdinand	Marengo	Seelyville
Beech Grove	Fishers	Marion	Sheridan
Beverly Shores	Floyds Knobs	McCordsville	Shipshewana
Bloomfield	Fortville	Merrillville	South Bend
Bloomington	Fort Wayne	Middlebury	Speedway
Brazil	Fountain City	Mishawaka	Spencer
Brookston	Frankfort	Monon	Story
Brookville	Franklin	Montgomery	Syracuse
Brownsburg	Fremont	Mooresville	Terre Haute
Carmel	French Lick	Morristown	Thorntown
Cambridge City	Gas City	Mulberry	Topeka
Cedar Lake	Goshen	Muncie	Upland
Centerville	Greencastle	Munster	Unionville
Chesterton	Greenfield	Nashville	Valparaiso
Cicero	Greenville	New Albany	Vincennes
Clarksville	Hagerstown	Newburgh	Wabash
Columbus	Haubstadt	New Castle	Warsaw
Commiskey	Hobart	New Harmony	West Baden Springs
Connersville	Hope	Nineveh	Westfield
Corydon	Huntertown	Noblesville	Whitestown
Covington	Huntington	North Salem	Winchester
Crawfordsville	Indianapolis	Oldenburg	WInona Lake
Crown Point	Jasper	Paoli	Wolcottville
Culver	Jeffersonville	Pendleton	Worthington
Daleville	Jonesville	Perkinsville	Zionsville
Dana	Kendallville	Peru	Zulu
Danville	Kentland	Plymouth	
Decatur	Knightstown	Porter	
Delphi	Kokomo	Poseyville	

Easy to Use

Dining Secrets is designed to be used as you travel around the state. There are over 375 listings for places to eat, visit and indulge.

ALPHABETICAL LISTING BY TOWN

The front index is organized alphabetically by city or town. As you travel Indiana, search the "City/Town" column to find the location you are in or nearby. Each restaurant listing includes the phone number and page number for reference.

RESTAURANT INFORMATION

Restaurants are listed alphabetically by name. Each entry includes the address, phone number, days of operation and meals served. A website is listed when available. IT IS ALWAYS ADVISABLE TO CALL AHEAD FOR SPECIFIC TIMES AND CONFIRMATION.

TOUR INDIANA

Monuments, museums, activites, and places of interest are listed by town. Contact information is available for easy reference.

SWEETS AND TREATS

A new section of DINING SECRETS™ suggests places to stop for a quick snack or treat while traveling, or a destination place to pick up highly recommended specialty items.

ALPHABETICAL INDEX BY RESTAURANT

To search for a specific restaurant, the index in the back of DINING SECRETS™ lists restaurants alphabetically by name and page number.

Every effort has been made to present accurate information. However, changes do occur and it is always recommended that you call ahead for confirmation.

Poole Publishing chose the restaurants to be included in DINING SECRETS™ and did not charge any fee or accept any services from the restaurants.

New restaurant ideas are always of interest.
Contact Poole Publishing, (317) 849-9199 or kspoole@sbcglobal.net

Alphabetical Index by Town

If you would like additional copies of "DINING SECRETS™ *of* Indiana", *check with your local bookstore, gift shop, "Dining Secrets" restaurant, or contact Poole Publishing.*

DINING SECRETS™
of
Indiana

POOLE PUBLISHING
(317) 849-9199
kspoole@sbcglobal.net

Restaurants

3 DAYS IN PARIS
222 East Market Street
Indianapolis, IN 46204
(317) 912-0072
www.3daysinpariscrepes.com
Open Monday-Saturday for breakfast & lunch. Closed Sunday.

You can visit the Indianapolis City Market year round. Wander into the old market-place and check out the line viewing the crepe-making activity at 3 Days in Paris. The batter is mixed, poured on the skillet, flipped at just the right moment, sweet or savory ingredients added, and then folded for immediate consumption. You might grab a cup of freshly roasted coffee while you walk around shopping or find a seat upstairs overlooking all the market activity. 3 Days in Paris has a presence and a loyal following at seasonal local markets.

3 FLOYDS BREWERY
9750 Indiana Parkway
Munster, IN 46321
(219) 922-3565
www.3floyds.com
Open daily for lunch & dinner.

A visit to 3 Floyds Brewery is quite an experience. People come from all over to eat, drink and buy beer. The atmosphere is busy: beer being brewed as diners watch from window seats; beer being poured from multiple taps at the bar; and food being delivered to tables of hungry customers. 3 Floyds serves year-round, seasonal and pub-only brews. Numerous tap handles decorate the walls. You might assume the food is an afterthought, but it is a total surprise. Who would expect a menu that includes a small plate of octopus bulgogi, a basil pesto pizza, wood-grilled trout or a side of alpha fries? Be sure to wave to the Alpha King statue out front when you leave.

10 WEST RESTAURANT & BAR
10 West Jackson Street
Cicero, IN 46034
(317) 606-8542
Open Tuesday-Saturday for dinner. Closed Sunday & Monday.

Located in the heart of Cicero, this family-friendly tavern has a cozy, casual atmosphere, created by a combination of exposed brick walls, limestone bar, comfortable booths, and subdued lighting. A focal point in the main dining area is the community table that seats 12, custom-made from an 18-foot poplar tree. Appetizers include the standard fare, but you might try the grilled cheese crostini served with tomato horseradish soup for dipping. In addition to nightly specials, there is a nice selection of steaks, seafood, pastas, burgers and sandwiches, along with flatbread pizzas and "Twisted Tacos." You can also dine in the Cellar, complete with fireplace and grand piano, or just enjoy some cocktails and munchies while listening to live music on certain evenings.

33 BRICK STREET

480 South Maple Street
French Lick, IN 47432
(812) 936-3370
www.33brickstreet.com
Open Tuesday-Sunday for lunch & dinner; Monday for dinner.

The restaurant was opened to help revitalize downtown French Lick. A Baden Springs-born friend, Larry Bird (#33), agreed to loan some of his sports memorabilia and collectibles to decorate this sports bar. Along with neon beer signs and other sports relics, there is a lot of interest in Bird's jerseys, trophies and championship rings. Craft beers, daily fresh-cut steaks, burgers and homemade soups highlight the menu along with Friday, Saturday and Sunday dinner specials. A Half Time Lunch menu is available for lighter luncheon fare.

ADAM'S LAKE PUB

5365 East 620 South
Wolcottville, IN 46795
(260) 854-3463
www.adamslakepub.com
Open Wednesday-Sunday for dinner. Closed Monday & Tuesday.

The northeastern corner of Indiana has several lakes and this restaurant is located on one of them. Sitting outside on the deck in front of this attractive stone structure is seasonally ideal. Inside, there is an extensive well-stocked bar and additional seating around a fireplace. Fresh seafood is promised along with steaks, pork and chicken. Friendly local staff might suggest "Brew City beer-battered black and tan onion rings" to accompany your entree. Sandwiches and salads are also available.

AINSLEY'S CAFÉ & HARBOR BAR

15179 Old State Road 101
Brookville, IN 47012
(765) 458-7474
www.ainsleylakeside.com
Open for lunch & dinner seasonally. CALL AHEAD.

If you have never been to the Brookville area of Indiana, you are in for a treat. All the typical lake amenities are available, including hiking, swimming, fishing, camping and relaxing. If you are out on the water, you can get to Ainsley's by boat and dock at Kent's Harbor Marina. Dining either inside or outside on the huge screened deck affords a relaxing view of the lake and the Harbor Links Golf Course. The menu has something for everyone, including children. The stack of onion straws, cooked-to-order steaks, and catfish have received good recommendations.

ALMOST HOME

17 West Franklin Street
Greencastle, IN 46135
(765) 653-5788
www.almosthomerestaurant.com
Open daily for lunch & dinner.

Window boxes filled with wildflowers decorate the entrance to this charming restaurant specializing in delicious homemade soups, croissant sandwiches, salads and delectable desserts, plus a dinner menu with wonderful flavors. Beer and wine are also available. The homey interior is a comfortable spot for friends to meet for a relaxing meal. You will enjoy browsing in the gift shop featuring a unique collection of antiques and vintage furniture, a vast selection of gifts for any occasion, home decor items, and collectibles. Surrounded by friendly   people in a bright and cheery setting, you feel as if you are "almost home."

AL-RAYAN RESTAURANT

4873 West 38th Street
Indianapolis, IN 46254
(317) 986-7554
www.alrayanrestaurant.com
Open daily for breakfast, lunch & dinner.

Sit on the floor in a curtained booth or at a table in this Middle Eastern-Mediterranean restaurant serving food in the Yemini tradition. The best way to enjoy the meal is to have a taste of everything: hummus, kabobs, lamb chops, fahsa (shredded lamb in a clay pot), chicken and beef. It is a fun meal to share with a group as all of the items mentioned are served on top of Basmati rice on a huge circular tray. Pita bread and a salad called fatoosh perfectly complement the main dishes. Al-Rayan is a family operated restaurant in the International Marketplace of Indianapolis. Adjacent to the restaurant is a bakery and other stores owned by the family.

ART'S SKILLET

8255 Pendleton Pike
Indianapolis, IN 46226
(317) 672-2367
www.artsskillet.com
Open daily for breakfast, brunch and lunch.

Art's Skillet is the result of an American dream coming true. Art found himself unemployed and decided to act upon his entrepreneurial ambitions. Using his years of experience in the food industry, he opened a restaurant serving an omelette that one "Dining Secrets" user advertised as "the best." The omelette choices are, in fact, outstanding with about every ingredient imaginable. The skillet options are also far reaching: Bohemian, German, Irish and others. Peasant potatoes are a side, along with a choice of breads and French toast. If it's not breakfast time, sandwiches and salads are also on the menu.

ASIAN GRILL

74 North 9th Street
Noblesville, IN 46060
(317) 773-9990
www.asiangrillnoblesville.com
Open daily for lunch & dinner.

Housed on the square in Noblesville, the late 1800s store has been redesigned to showcase the original wood floors while also looking sleek and contemporary. Asian Grill serves unique cuisines from Cambodia, China, India, Japan, Thailand and Vietnam. In addition to traditional appetizers, there is a vegetable samosa and vegetable pakora with special ingredients. The entrées are another story. Once you decide between chicken, beef, seafood, vegetarian or noodles, you then begin the difficult task of choosing which combination of vegetables and spices sounds the best to you. Asian beers and wines from many lands are available to complement your meal.

ASPARAGUS

7876 Broadway
Merrillville, IN 46410
(219) 794-0000
www.asparagusrestaurant.com
Open daily for lunch & dinner.

The promise at the top of the menu is, "Thai-Vietnamese-French, where innovation and fusion reign." Whether you choose an appetizer, soup, satay, salad, noodles, rice, or meat, the menu tantalizes the taste buds with its mixture of spices and flavors: curry, ginger, cilantro, saffron, lemongrass, etc. The seafood selections are numerous and, of course, asparagus is available with many entrées. You may enjoy appetizers at a table in the martini bar or in one of the other dining rooms. Fresh flowers decorate the tables.

ATHENS ON 86TH STREET

2284 West 86th Street
Indianapolis, IN 46260
(317) 879-8644
Open Tuesday-Sunday for lunch & dinner. Closed Monday.

A friendly atmosphere greets you as you enter this Greek restaurant. The Norwegian/ Greek owners have used structural columns and lots of open space to create an environment that feels like an upscale European café. There is also outdoor seating, weather permitting, and a banquet room for large groups. The table staff takes pleasure in helping you choose your meal. The familiar Greek specialties like spanikopita, gyros, mousaka, dolmathes and kabobs are available, but you should treat yourself to something new, such as yemista, lahanodolmathes, or gigantes. Of course, there is fileto, pork chops and lamb chops for the less adventurous diner. Off-site catering is available.

AUBURN'S TOWN TAVERN

1343 South Main Street
Auburn, IN 46706
(260) 925-0555
Open Monday-Saturday for breakfast, lunch & dinner; Sunday for breakfast & lunch.

When driving to Michigan or visiting one of the area museums (see "Tour Indiana" section), you must eat at this hundred-year-old restaurant where breakfast used to cost just 15 cents. No matter what meal you are stopping for, delicious food is served in this unassuming family-style bar/tavern. For breakfast, you may choose the City Boy or Farm Girl or settle for the Mess or Garbage Scrambler. Diners come from miles around to eat the deep fried Alaskan pollock prepared with a secret recipe breading as a lunch sandwich or dinner entrée.

BACK FORTY JUNCTION

1011 North 13th Street
Decatur, IN 46733
(260) 724-3355
Open daily for lunch & dinner.

This establishment opened in the early 1950s and is "one big antique, from one end to the other," according to the manager. A restored caboose from circa 1800, along with a 1920s club car and many other railroad artifacts, sits outside. Tiffany lamps, as well as a lamp from Carole Lombard's home, light the interior. Burma Shave signs decorate the cathedral ceiling, and there are 15 John Rogers sculptures depicting detailed scenes of everyday American life in the 1800s lining one wall. The buffet-style fare offers the traditional selections of steak, ribs and chicken, but the highlights are the prime rib carved daily and the all-you-can-eat crab legs on Friday nights.

BAKERSFIELD MASS AVE

334 Massachusetts Avenue
Indianapolis, IN 46204
(317) 635-6962
www.bakersfieldtacos.com
Open daily for lunch & dinner.

If tacos, tequila and whiskey are what you are looking for, Bakersfield is a destination. With seats looking out on Mass Avenue, this upscale saloon offers "Mexican street fare" to accompany your drink. Lively music plays as you order one of a variety of tacos, tostadas or tortas on telera rolls (similar to ciabatta). Customers have positive comments about the guacamole and chips and the corn chowder.

BARTLETT'S

131 East Dunes Highway 12
Beverly Shores, IN 46301
(219) 879-3081
www.eatatbartletts.com
Open daily for lunch & dinner.

Driving toward the restaurant with its "deer drinking beer" logo reminds you of driving in the north woods of Wisconsin. The feeling continues as you walk into a knotty pine dining room with an inviting little bar tucked away in the corner. Assorted photos and paintings by local artists adorn the walls. Cheese and crackers are delivered to your table, along with a list of the daily specials. Menu items that catch the eye are deviled eggs, fennel apple coleslaw, five hour pot roast, white mac and cheese, dry spice rubbed baby back ribs and parmesan chicken chili. You can also take out food for a picnic at the nearby beach.

BAZBEAUX PIZZA

329 Massachusetts Avenue
Indianapolis, IN 46204
(317) 636-7662
www.bazbeaux.com
Open daily for lunch & dinner.

Bazbeaux was the whimsical name given to a court jester, whose cleverness was used to create new dishes to amuse the courts he served. In 1986, the Bazbeaux legend was brought to Indianapolis as the first restaurant in the area to introduce pizza lovers to a new concept: unique combinations of sometimes exotic toppings on a choice of wheat or white crust. Building on the success of the Broad Ripple location, they expanded to an old downtown building in the art and theater district and are now located across the street. Lunch specials include pizza by the slice. Pizza alla quattro formaggio is the most popular—five cheeses, bacon and mushrooms. The muffaletta and stromboli sandwiches are also in demand. Desserts are delicious too—try the popular tartufo or sorbetti. A nice selection of beer and wine is available. While you are there, look at the designs by local artists decorating the interior.

BEEF HOUSE

I-74 & State Road 63
Covington, IN 47932
(765) 793-3947
www.beefhouserolls.com
Open daily for lunch & dinner.

The Wright family purchased a small restaurant in 1963 and became well-known for their homemade rolls, a recipe secured at Purdue University while majoring in hotel/restaurant management. Today, they continue to be famous for the fact that all of the food served is homemade, including wonderful soups and delicious pies. If you are in the mood for a terrific steak, made from high choice aged beef, this is the place to go. You may also enjoy one of their dinner theater shows—call for information.

BILLY'S

18000 Lincoln Highway East
Zulu (Monroeville), IN 46773
(260) 623-3583
Open Wednesday-Sunday for dinner. Closed Monday & Tuesday.

Tell your friends you want to take them to dinner at a bar in downtown Zulu! Yes, when naming the town, a globe was spun and the finger landed on Zulu in Africa. Plaid booths, a statue of the Blues Brothers, a juke box, sports memorabilia, and the "Wall of Shame or is it Fame" collages all combine to create an inviting atmosphere. Popular menu items include the broiled or fried haddock, filet, T-bone and pork chops, or you may prefer the Mexican food choices of nachos, burritos, or flautas.

BIRD'S SMOKEHOUSE BBQ

9008 South Walnut Street
Daleville, IN 47334
(765) 378-1900
www.birdssmokehousebbq.com
Open daily for lunch & dinner.

A line that describes the history of the restaurant and its logo is, "Dare to dream the impossible—pigs really do fly!" The Smokehouse started out in a wagon that parked on corners at local festivals, but Bird and Linda Strange's dream was to own a restaurant. Today, if you are driving on Interstate 69 and have a taste for slow cooked, smoked barbecue, pull off at the Daleville exit and look for the pink-winged pig high on the roof. Menu choices are pork, chicken or beef—pulled, on the bone or in a sandwich. Southern sides include corn casserole, southern green beans, and mashed potatoes with gravy. Chicken and noodles is the special on Sunday and Monday, plus salads and giant loaded spuds are available daily.

BISTRO 501

501 Main Street
Lafayette, IN 47901
(765) 423-4501
www.bistro501.com
Open Tuesday-Friday for lunch & dinner;
Monday & Saturday for dinner; Sunday for lunch.

On a corner in downtown Lafayette, this bright and cheery restaurant invites the passerby to come inside. Sunflowers and roosters fill the nooks and crannies of the dining room, adding to the pleasant atmosphere. The menu lists the usual appetizers, salads, sandwiches and entrées, but there is a lot of imagination in both the preparation and presentation that makes the food unique. Examples are the summer peach salad with berries and sunflower seeds, blackberry barbecued pork ribs, or huckleberry salmon. Featured entrées appear each week.

BLUEBEARD RESTAURANT

653 Virginia Avenue
Indianapolis, IN 46203
(317) 686-1580
www.bluebeardindy.com
Open Monday-Friday for lunch & dinner; Saturday & Sunday for dinner.

The underlying premise at Bluebeard is "food is meant for sharing." You can pick snacks, charcuterie, cheese, soups, salads, sandwiches and/or entrées of differing sizes. The menu varies daily and updates are best accessed on the website. Be prepared to have a mouthwatering experience when you view the online photos. The restaurant is located in a renovated 1924 factory warehouse and includes a bar, dining room, and a courtyard that is desirable in good weather. Amelia's hearth-baked bread is made daily and is available at Bluebeard.

BLUE GATE RESTAURANT

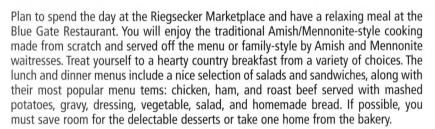

195 North Van Buren
Shipshewana, IN 46565
(260) 768-4725
www.riegsecker.com
Open Monday-Thursday for lunch & dinner;
Friday & Saturday for breakfast, lunch & dinner. Closed Sunday.

Plan to spend the day at the Riegsecker Marketplace and have a relaxing meal at the Blue Gate Restaurant. You will enjoy the traditional Amish/Mennonite-style cooking made from scratch and served off the menu or family-style by Amish and Mennonite waitresses. Treat yourself to a hearty country breakfast from a variety of choices. The lunch and dinner menus include a nice selection of salads and sandwiches, along with their most popular menu tems: chicken, ham, and roast beef served with mashed potatoes, gravy, dressing, vegetable, salad, and homemade bread. If possible, you must save room for the delectable desserts or take one home from the bakery.

BOATHOUSE

700 Park Avenue
Winona Lake, IN 46590
(574) 268-2179
www.boathouseatwinona.com
Open daily for lunch and dinner.

The original boathouse was built in 1895; today there is a new structure that was built in 2000 on the same site. History tells us that, in between, there was a cafeteria for the Winona Lake Bible Conference and a roller rink. Sit in a comfortable booth and enjoy a menu that includes chicken, seafood, steaks and pasta dishes, along with salads and sandwiches. The choices reflect the freshest available ingredients and are creatively prepared: boom boom shrimp, ravioli español, pretzel crusted walleye, pasta bruschetta, makhani chicken and smoked pork chops. Seasonally, outside seating is most desirable. For a before or after treat, the Winona Mercantile is adjacent to the restaurant and has a variety of unique gift items.

BONGE'S TAVERN

9830 West 280N
Perkinsville, IN 46011
(765) 734-1625
www.bongestavern.com
Open Tuesday-Saturday for dinner. Closed Sunday & Monday.

Bonge's Tavern put this small town on the map as people literally flock to Perkinsville to eat in this old converted hardware store. You might have to wait on the porch or outdoors if the weather is nice, but it is well worth the trip. The owners took pride in creating the rustic-style restaurant and recommend you take a look at the memorabilia displayed throughout, including the pinball machine tops hanging on the wall in the private dining area. The menu changes regularly, and there is a variety of blackboard specials, but the popular Perkinsville pork is always on the menu. Some who visit Bonge's restrooms write a message on the wall. Be sure to check it out!

BOSPHORUS ISTANBUL CAFÉ

935 South East Street
Indianapolis, IN 46225
(317) 974-1770
www.bosphoruscafe.us
Open Monday-Saturday for lunch & dinner; Sunday for dinner.

The little clapboard house at this address has a sign that identifies it as Bosphorus Café; otherwise, it might not be clear that you have found Indianapolis' first Turkish restaurant. As you step inside, however, the music, the painted floors, the pictures, the people and the menu assure you that you are at the right place. Turkish names are given to the various food items, but good English explanations are printed on the menu. Appetizers include hummus, eggplant salsa and falafel. Kebabs, stuffed eggplant, and gyros are familiar choices but if you are feeling adventurous, try Ispanklitavuk (spinach chicken) or Iskender (slices of doner on grilled bread cubes with tomato sauce). Seafood specialties and veggie dishes are also available, and you might want to try the Ayran, an interesting Turkish yogurt drink.

BOULDER CREEK DINING COMPANY

1551 North Green Street
Brownsburg, IN 46112
(317) 858-8100
www.bouldercreekdining.com
Open daily for lunch & dinner.

Dine outside in good weather or inside amidst a forested environment. There are tree trunks, twig mirrors, and picturesque outdoor settings to set the mood for dining. Whether visiting for lunch or dinner, the menu offers predictable choices: appetizers, sandwiches, pizzas, salads and main courses. What is special is the preparation of the items like campfire fettuccine, Hoosier pizza, pueblo chicken and horseradish-dijon crusted sirloin.

BRASS RAIL BAR & GRILL

225 North Michigan
Plymouth, IN 46563
(574) 936-7004
www.thebrassrailbarandgrill.com
Open Monday-Saturday for lunch & dinner. Closed Sunday.

Traveling through Northern Indiana on your way "to or from," the Brass Rail is a good family-owned restaurant to stop for a bite to eat. In addition to traditional lunch sandwiches, there are ciabatta and pretzel bread/bun choices. Stuffed baked potatoes and salads are also available. The most requested specialty is the hand-breaded cod cooked in cholesterol-free shortening. The dinner menu expands to include steaks, salmon specialties, lake perch, and alfredo pasta choices. Yes, there is a real brass rail in this comfortable corner bar and restaurant.

BRAU HAUS

22170 Water Street
Oldenburg, IN 47036
(812) 934-4840
www.oldenburgbrauhaus.com
Open Tuesday-Sunday for lunch & dinner.
Closed Monday.

Listed on the National Register of Historic Places, the town of Oldenburg is also known as the "Village of Spires," a vivid example of the old world German heritage in America. The restaurant's menu is filled with many traditional lunch and dinner items, such as homemade soups, sandwiches, steaks and seafood. The specialties are the Brau Haus chicken and Oldenburg's Favorites: the Brau Haus reuben, homemade sausage pattie dinner, and fresh bratwurst with sauerkraut on rye. If you are in the area, you might enjoy combining a stop at the Brau Haus with a tour of this historic village.

BREAD BASKET CAFÉ & BAKERY

46 South Tennessee Street
Danville, IN 46122
(317) 718-4800
www.breadbasketcafe.com
Open Tuesday-Saturday for breakfast & lunch. Closed Sunday & Monday.

Picture yourself opening the door to a lovely white house in a small town and being greeted by the overwhelming aroma of freshly baked breads, pies and cookies. Tables of all different shapes and sizes, decorated with fresh flowers and colorful placemats, are available in several dining rooms, including one accented with a fireplace. There are many tasty breakfast choices, such as cinnamon roll French toast, quiche, and apricot pistachio granola. For lunch, a unique addition to the favorite sandwiches is a B.L.T.E.A. (fried egg & avocado). Cranberry poppy seed chicken salad and orchard salad are also great options. Freshly made desserts are hard to ignore, and a fully stocked bakery enables you to take home reminders of a trip to the Bread Basket Café.

BRICK

309 Walnut Street
Jonesville, IN 47247
(812) 522-8636
Open Monday-Saturday for lunch & dinner. Closed Sunday.

The Brick is an anomaly in that it deviates from the normal <u>Dining Secrets</u> restaurant, but comes highly recommended. It is difficult to know you have arrived since the building is unassuming, the sign is inconspicuous, and the railroad track is so close it appears to be going through the structure. As you enter the restaurant, it is obvious that smoking is permitted and it's packed with lots of people. One reader commented, "A weekday lunch can be fun: farmers in bib overalls, suits from Columbus industries, bikers, etc." While enjoying the self-serve popcorn, you can view the "chef" carefully cooking thick, delicious hamburgers on a grill, adding toppings like onions and pickles, then wrapping them in wax paper (no plates) to be delivered to your table. The limited menu (no french fries) includes soups and chili.

BROZINNI PIZZERIA

8810 South Emerson
Indianapolis, IN 46237
(317) 865-0911
www.brozinni.net
Open daily for lunch and dinner.

You find yourself in suburban Greenwood, surrounded by pictures of New York City: the Brooklyn Bridge, the Statue of Liberty, Central Park's "Imagine" memorial to the Beatles, and more. The owner wanted to bring New York City pizza to Indiana, but there's question as to whether pizza in NYC is as good as Brozinni's. Homemade dough is used to make the breads, the knuckles, the calzones and of course, the pizza. Toppings that carry New York City names can be chosen to cover the tasty crisp crust. Pasta entrées are also available. If you are in the area, you can walk in and pick up a slice of yummy pizza right out of the oven.

BRUGGE BRASSERIE

1011 East Westfield Boulevard
Indianapolis, IN 46220
(317) 255-0978
www.bruggebrasserie.com
Open daily for lunch & dinner. Brunch on Saturday & Sunday.

Brugge is all about mussels (moules), fries (frites), beer and Belgium. The mussels are delivered in a pot and you choose from 12 different ways you would like them prepared: cajun, tomato lemon cream, and Asian are just a few possibilities. Cones of french fries that fit into holes in the table are not served simply with homemade ketchup. Instead, there are 12 different dips, including herb pesto, blue cheese and hot curry. Sandwiches, small plates and crepes with seasonal ingredients are also offered, but be sure to include some fries with your order. Dessert crepes are a good choice to complete your meal.

BRUNO'S

212 Brown Street
West Lafayette, IN 47106
(765) 743-1668
www.brunodough.com
Open daily for dinner.

A well-known landmark to Boilermaker fans, this Swiss Italian restaurant is filled with memorabilia. The walls tell stories about local athletes who have gone on to play professionally. In fact, Bob Griese and Len Dawson are among the famous visitors. The pizza kitchen is in plain view as you enter the restaurant, and the pizza is still unbeatable. Bruno Dough is the recommended appetizer—golf ball size pieces of deep-fried pizza dough, brushed with garlic butter and served with meat or cheese sauce. Homemade lasagna, pasta dinners, and a variety of veal, pork and chicken dishes round out the Italian menu. The Swiss influence can be found in choices of wiener schnitzel, cheese fondue, bratwurst and knackwurst. Interestingly, catfish has also become a favorite at this restaurant.

BUB'S BURGERS & ICE CREAM

210 West Main Street
Carmel, IN 46032
(317) 706-2827
www.bubsburgersandicecream.com
Open daily for lunch & dinner.

Bub's is a Monon Trail destination and is a wonderful reason to take a walk. Yes, Bub is the owner's nickname, but it also stands for "Big Ugly Burger." The "Big Ugly" is a one pound handpattied burger and there is a Wall of Champions with pictures of those who have eaten one. For the less ambitious, there is the half-pound "Not So Ugly" or the quarter-pound "Settle for Less Ugly." The ugly burgers come on custom made rolls and can be accompanied by waffle fries, onion rings, or regular fries. There is an elk burger on the menu for low-fat conscious customers. If burgers aren't your thing, other options include Black Angus hot dogs, chili, chicken and Bub's grilled Mahi Mahi sandwiches. Soups are served in bread bowls. Colorful farm scene murals decorate the interior of the ice cream shop in the front of the building. Import/specialty beers and wines are available.

BUSH

932 Locust Street
Terre Haute, IN 47807
(812) 238-1148
www.thebushrestaurant.com
Open Monday-Saturday for lunch & dinner. Closed Sunday.

The "lure" of this restaurant is the cod fish sandwiches. Located next to the railroad tracks, the local people have been gathering here for well over 50 years, documented by the photos on the walls. Look for the pictures of Howdy Doody & Bob and Hopalong Cassidy. The breading for the cod and the tenderloin is homemade and delicious. You can order a baby or jumbo fish sandwich and a whole or half tenderloin with sides of 'shrooms, rings, cole slaw, french fries, or hush puppies. Pasta, salad, burgers, chicken, ribeye steak and catfish are also available, but cod is the specialty.

CAFÉ ARAZU

17 West Jennings Street
Newburgh, IN 47630
(812) 842-2200
www.cafe-arazu.com
Open Monday-Saturday for lunch & dinner. Closed Sunday.

The philosophy behind Café Arazu is to present "world cuisines with a neighborhood feel." As you enter the cozy ethnic restaurant with flowing Middle Eastern silk and bead decorations, you find yourself enveloped in the owner's goal. Her desire is to provide a gathering place for people of different cultures to meet and celebrate what they have in common, rather than "stew over their differences." Appetizers include different kinds of hummus, eggplant dip and bruschetta. Salads feature handmade dressings. For lunch, there is chicken shawarma, falafel burger and Tuscan grilled beef salad. Dinner choices include shish kebabs, fresh wild caught salmon, tandoori chicken, plus sandwiches and pita platters.

CAFÉ at BATAR

12649 Highway 50 East
Seymour, IN 47274
(812) 522-8617
www.cafebatar.blogspot.com
Open Wednesday-Saturday for lunch. Closed Sunday-Tuesday.
Closed mid-December; re-opens mid-March.

As you step outside your car, take a deep breath–the scent will make you feel like you are surrounded by a pine forest. Actually, you are right next to the Muscatatuck National Wildlife Refuge. Sitting amidst the natural beauty is Café Batar, the Parlor Music Museum, and the Batar Gift Shop. Lunch is served in this quaint café, filled with windows overlooking the colorful gardens visited by hummingbirds and butterflies. Antique wedgewood china is used to serve sandwiches, soups, salads and wraps, along with the weekly specials. Of course, the emphasis is on dessert with strawberry creme cake and raspberry chocolate cake among the popular choices, but Bun-Apple Tite is the specialty. After lunch, take some time to wander the garden and visit the gift shop and museum with a Life magazine collection spanning decades.

CAFÉ AT SINCLAIR'S

West Baden Springs Hotel
8538 West Baden Avenue
West Baden Springs, IN 47469
(812) 936-5579
Open daily for dinner.

Once considered the Eighth Wonder of the World, the West Baden Springs Hotel has been restored to its former glorious state. Seeing the domed atrium (reportedly the world's largest dome) is a treat in itself. The attention to detail in the renovation of the hotel is absolutely remarkable. Sinclair's, named for one of the original owners, is furnished with the same care. The overall look is formal with white tablecloths, dark woodwork, classic furniture and an abundance of glass. The dinner menu is filled with culinary delights such as sweet lobster fettuccine, rack of lamb, stuffed baby eggplant, and filet mignon. No matter what you choose, eating in this fairy-tale hotel will be an extraordinary experience.

CAFE AUDREY at the Fort

9134 Otis Avenue
Indianapolis, IN 46216
(317) 546-6000
www.cafeaudreyatfortben.com
Open Sunday-Wednesday for breakfast & lunch; Thursday-Saturday for breakfast, lunch & dinner.

The U.S. Army's Fort Benjamin Harrison is located on the northeast side of Indianapolis. Cafe Audrey is housed in the Fort's old blacksmith shop where the ceiling and floor are clearly the original. Vintage signs and old pictures decorate the walls, but a sign that reaches out to all of the restaurant's customers is, "Enter as strangers. Leave as friends." Daily specials are listed on the blackboard, but the regular menu has some mouth-watering entries like cinnamon roll pancakes, eggnog brioche French toast, kale slaw, gourmet egg salad, and a Reuben-like sandwich made with turkey. You can serve yourself "bottomless cups" of coffee and tea.

CAMMACK STATION

9200 West Jackson Street
Muncie, IN 47304
(765) 759-3871
Open daily for lunch & dinner.

The address is Muncie, but the historic town of Cammack is the actual location. The old gas station, complete with service bays, has been converted to a restaurant and is decorated with old gas pumps, license plates, Coca Cola signs, and other filling station memorabilia. Orders for hamburgers, fried bologna, tenderloins, coney dogs, onion rings and fountain drinks are placed at the counter. The station boasts being the home of the famous Blue Bell ice cream and prides itself on its desserts. While in town, you might walk around and note the old farm and fire equipment parked along the roadside.

CAPLINGER'S FRESH CATCH SEAFOOD MARKET

7460 North Shadeland Avenue
Indianapolis, IN 46250
(317) 288-7263
www.caplingersfreshcatch.com
Open Tuesday-Saturday for lunch & dinner. Closed Sunday & Monday.

A large selection of fresh fish is what draws you to Caplinger's, and you order at the counter to dine in or carry out. You can also walk in and purchase fresh fish to prepare at home. There are lobster rolls and handmade crab cakes, but don't overlook the Caplinger Special. For dinner, fresh fish from the cooler can be grilled or fried and accompanied by a variety of tasty sides: collard greens, red beans & rice, hush puppies, cole slaw, and green beans. Homemade desserts of key lime pie and pineapple bread pudding are available to top off your meal. The menu states that "whatever you may be looking for that swims, we can probably find it if we don't already carry it."

CAPRI RISTORANTE ITALIANO

2602 Ruth Drive (74th & North Keystone)
Indianapolis, IN 46240
(317) 259-4122
www.capriindy.com
Open Monday-Friday for lunch & dinner; Saturday & Sunday for dinner.

The interior has a warm and inviting atmosphere with two different dining areas to suit your mood or occasion. The formal dining room has fresh flowers, high ceilings, and soft lighting; the cozy bar, complete with fireplace, is a more relaxed setting. The owner is Italian and many of his creations are prepared from family recipes. The pasta is homemade and outstanding dishes are filled with ingredients that showcase the chef's imagination. For the main course, there is always a fresh fish of the day, but you may want veal, chicken or a filet instead.

CAPTAIN'S CABIN

3070 West Shadyside Road
Angola, IN 46703
(260) 665-5663
www.captainscabinrestaurant.com
Open Wednesday-Saturday for dinner.

There is quite a history surrounding this old log cabin that has been serving diners for over 50 years. The log walls and ceilings, wooden captain's chairs, and candles on every table add to the rustic charm. The atmosphere is casual, but it is truly a fine dining establishment. In fact, the owners claim, "The only thing we overlook is Crooked Lake." Relax and enjoy the spectacular lake view while dining on superb lobster, seafood or a choice steak dinner. The Captain's Cabin Lounge offers a warm atmosphere for after dinner conversation.

CARNEGIE'S

100 West North Street
Greenfield, IN 46140
(317) 462-8480
www.carnegiesrestaurant.blogspot.com
Open Tuesday-Saturday for dinner. Closed Sunday & Monday.

The downstairs area of the former Carnegie library provides a unique, inviting and cozy setting for diners to enjoy their meal. Dark green walls create the perfect backdrop for the artwork displayed throughout the restaurant. While dining at Carnegie's, you must take a tour of the herb gardens and see the outdoor Roman-style wood-fired oven used for baking breads. The chef offers a menu that changes with the seasons and focuses on gourmet dishes presented as an art form. Creative dinner entrées feature ossobuco (veal shank), duck breast, salmon and pork tenderloin. Carnegie's offers catering, and the upper floor is available for parties.

CARRIAGE HOUSE

24460 Adams Road
South Bend, IN 46628
(574) 272-9220
www.carriagehousedining.com
Open Tuesday-Saturday for dinner. Closed Sunday & Monday.

Built in 1851 as a Brethren church emphasizing the simplistic, it is difficult to imagine the history as you step inside this elegantly appointed restaurant. Along with classical music in the background, the antiques and tasteful accessories decorating the interior provide a pleasant environment for this fine dining experience. Begin the meal with a choice of cold or warm appetizers: steak tartare, smoked salmon, Mediterranean grape leaves or rabbit sausage. Outstanding entrées include Beef Wellington, rack of lamb, steaks, veal and seafood. As recipients of the <u>Wine Spectator</u> "Best" Award, you can be assured of an extensive wine list. Excellence is clearly the goal here.

CARUSO'S RESTAURANT

2435 North 200 West
Angola, IN 46703
(260) 833-2617
www.carusos-restaurant.com
Open Tuesday-Saturday for lunch & dinner; Sunday seasonal. Closed Monday.

Caruso's has been serving house-made classic Italian cuisine since 1976 and is looked upon as an institution in the northeast Indiana lakes region. Whether you choose pizza, pasta or Classico Italiano chicken or veal, you can be assured that only imported pastas and extra virgin olive oil from Italy are used to prepare the authentic Italian dishes. A unique menu item is Caruso's famous "Torpedoughs" that comes with a choice of six different stuffings. The menu also includes paninis, salads and soups. Fridays feature a fresh fish recipe, and cowboy ribeyes are always available. You might enjoy dining on the patio in nice weather.

CATABLU GRILLE

6372 West Jefferson Blvd.
Fort Wayne, IN 46804
(260) 456-6563
www.thecatablugrille.com
Open Monday-Friday for lunch & dinner; Saturday for dinner. Closed Sunday.

Catablu was originally located in the downtown historic Cinema Blue Theater that the owners restored and then, in 2009, moved to the southwest side of Fort Wayne. The theater theme continues with movie quotes printed on the riser above the inviting semicircular bar. There is a huge wall of wine bottles, complete with a library-style ladder. The food is attractive to the eye and incorporates the latest trends in fresh and flavorful ingredients. There are even stir-fry, salad and sandwich offerings tailored to dietary preferences. Cold-pressed juices and seasonal martinis are also available.

CERULEAN RESTAURANT

1100 East Canal Street
Winona Lake, IN 46590
(574) 269-1226
www.ceruleanrestaurant.com
Open Monday-Saturday for lunch & dinner. Closed Sunday.

While in the northern Indiana lake region, you will enjoy visiting this restaurant for both the food and the atmosphere. You can dine on the porch overlooking the canal or in a well-appointed dining room where the decor entertains you with its colors and shapes. Japanese Bento Boxes are the lunch attraction; you select one main item like wasabi crusted shrimp, then choose three sides such as Asian noodles, mesclun salad, or edamame. For dinner, there is a list of mouthwatering tapas, pastas, meat and vegetarian choices, plus salads and soups. A complete menu of sushi, sashimi, and chef specialty rolls are always available. The desserts are excellent, too.

CHAPPELL'S CORAL GRILL

6328 West Jefferson Boulevard
Fort Wayne, IN 46804
(260) 456-9652
www.chappellseafood.com
Open Monday-Friday for lunch & dinner; Saturday for dinner. Closed Sunday.

Fish is the focus and comes to Chappell's from all over the world. The bar commands your attention, but eating in the comfortable, nautical-themed dining room is also appealing. Chicken, steak and pasta choices are on the menu, but there is every reason to order one of the seafood specials. They take pride in their bread crumb toppings, crusts, and flavorful sauces. The crab coleslaw is a special choice as a side dish.

CHICKEN HOUSE

7180 State Road 111
Sellersburg, IN 47172
(812) 246-9485
www.thechickenhouseonline.com
Open Monday-Saturday for dinner. Closed Sunday.

As you drive along State Road 111 through the farmland of Southern Indiana, you will come upon an old white house near the road with a sign saying "Restaurant." The local clientele in this "no frills" establishment say the house has been there for over 100 years, and most of the tables are reserved on a Saturday evening. People come for the fried chicken, but livers, gizzards, pan-fried oysters, and country ham are also available. The menu states that the food is prepared to order so it takes a little longer, but they pledge that "it is worth the extra time you wait."

CHOCOLATE MOOSE

101 North Main Street
Farmland, IN 47340
(765) 468-7731
Open Tuesday-Saturday for lunch & dinner. Closed Sunday & Monday.

The Chocolate Moose can best be described as an old-fashioned '50s soda bar, complete with Coke memorabilia, poodle skirts on display, and Elvis looking at you over the counter. There are sundaes, floats, sodas, hand-dipped milkshakes and ice creams of every flavor. Homemade sugar cream pie and strawberry shortcake are also on the treat list. Seasonal soups and salads, signature sandwiches like the Angry Bird, and burgers with different toppings are on the menu. While in Farmland, an Historic Places Town since 1994, walk down the street to the Farmland General Store where candies of all kinds, popular over generations, are displayed in glass cases. A huge selection of antiques is available next to the General Store.

CHOP'S STEAKS & SEAFOOD

6421 West Jefferson Boulevard
Fort Wayne, IN 46804
(260) 436-9115
www.chopswineanddine.com
Open Monday-Friday for lunch and dinner; Saturday for dinner; Sunday for brunch.

As you open the door, the splashes of color on the walls and the enthusiastic staff make you smile. The menu is pleasing with a lot of well-prepared chicken, steak and pasta entrées. For lunch, the grinder sandwiches and bruschetta chicken provide something a little different. Dinners are accompanied by a Chop salad and signature in-house baked bread. Chop's has a wine bar next door, the first in Fort Wayne, that offers small portions along with a significant selection of wines during evening hours. Choose either venue and you won't be disappointed.

CHRISTIE'S ON THE SQUARE
34 Public Square
Salem, IN 47167
(812) 883-9757
www.christiesonsalemsquare.com
Open daily for lunch.

While exploring the history and scenic recreational areas in and around Salem, treat yourself to a meal at Christie's. The owner has introduced some of her mother's favorite recipes, such as homemade noodles and yeast rolls. For lunch, there are tasty soups that change daily, salads, sandwiches, and even some "lite" options. Don't forget to check out the dessert choices, more of mom's favorite recipes..

CHUBBY TROUT
2730 B Cassopolis Street
Elkhart, IN 46514
(574) 264-5700
www.chubbytrout.com
Open Monday-Friday for lunch & dinner;
Saturday for dinner. Closed Sunday.

If you are in Northern Indiana looking for sushi, you might check out the Chubby Trout. The menu includes entrées "from the field" but options from "fishin' off the pier" also tantalize the taste buds. For appetizers, there are cajun fish nibbles and oysters chubb. With the restaurant's proximity to the lake, perch is appealing but there is walleye, salmon, mahi mahi and tuna, all prepared with tasty glazes. The Chubby Trout advertises "fun people and serious food."

CJ'S PUB
236 South Michigan Street
South Bend, IN 46601
(574) 233-5981
www.cjs-pub.com
Open Monday-Saturday for lunch and dinner. Closed Sunday.

In 1984, Ricky Joe, an entertainer, opened CJ's before the "biggest and best burger" was popular. Super Pub Burgers are the specialty. Create your own burger, signature super size (10 oz.) or cubby size (5 oz.), from a choice of combinations: cheese oozing, spicy, egg, or bacon and cheese. There are also hockey, 4-horsemen or Derby burgers. Obviously the burgers are the reason to stop here, but salads, sandwiches and a special recipe chili are also available. This is a bar, so Pub Munchies, like the Hoosier State Fair mini corn dogs, are also on the menu.

CLUB SODA

235 East Superior Street
Fort Wayne, IN 46802
(260) 426-3442
www.clubsodafortwayne.com
Open Monday-Saturday for lunch & dinner. Closed Sunday.

The old structure and brick walls of the Indiana Textile Company lend a lot of character to what is now an upscale dining establishment and old-school nightclub. Dine on the main floor, the loft, or outdoors during warm weather. There is live jazz on Friday and Saturday nights, and memorabilia from the original Rat Pack (Frank Sinatra, Sammy Davis, Jr. and Dean Martin) decorates the walls. The lunch menu features burgers, sandwiches, soups and salads. Dinner selections include Black Angus beef steak, prime rib, seafood, chicken, pork, duck and two or three daily specials. There is an extensive martini menu, from the classics to "the dark side," and a large, diverse wine list. Call ahead for reservations. You must be 21 to enter.

COLUMBUS BAR

322 Fourth Street
Columbus, IN 47201
(812) 375-8800
www.powerhousebrewingco.com
Open Monday-Saturday for lunch & dinner; Sunday for dinner.

Originally a blacksmith shop built in 1890, this historic downtown landmark has been operating as a restaurant since the 1960s. Some of the historical aspects have been maintained, particularly the antique neon sign out front and the inviting horseshoe-shaped bar modeled after a streetcar. You can enjoy fine handcrafted ales and guest beers from around the world. The private dining room offers a quieter, more relaxed environment and welcomes families with children. Menu highlights include the famous Columbus tenderloin, a mile high fish sandwich, and a reuben that has been hailed by many east coast guests as "authentic." Entrées like pork chops, chicken dinners and fish and chips are always available. This is a casual, friendly place to eat and mingle with the people of the community.

COMBINE CAFÉ

Reynolds Farm Equipment
1451 East 276th Street
Atlanta, IN 46031
(317) 758-4116
Open Monday-Saturday for breakfast & lunch. Closed Sunday.

This stop truly fits the "dining secret" criteria as it is tucked away in the Reynold's Farm Equipment showroom on U.S. Highway 31. It is a fun stop for breakfast or lunch. Farmers may be thought to like bacon, eggs and meat and potato-type food, but the menu here adds a special twist. The breakfast biscuits and gravy have jalapeño honey cheddar biscuits, and you can order eggs any way you like them. For lunch, the house roasted turkey sandwich comes on cranberry walnut bread with fig balsamic aioli. It is a great place to take the kids to see the child-sized farm equipment on display.

CONEY ISLAND WEINER STAND

131 West Main Street
Fort Wayne, IN 46802
(260) 424-2997
Open daily for lunch & dinner.

Coney Island Weiner Stand could be considered a Fort Wayne historical landmark. Since 1914, people have been walking in and ordering hot dogs at the counter: 5, 10, and 20 at a time; with onions, coney sauce, and/or mustard; to eat in or take out. The buns are lined up, hot dogs inserted, extras added, then wrapped and boxed to go. Coke comes in 8-ounce glass bottles. If you eat in, you can choose a stool at the counter or sit at the old porcelain topped tables. Historical photos of the restaurant and of Fort Wayne decorate the walls of this walk-in hot dog stand.

CORNDANCE

117 South Main Sttreet
South Bend, IN 46511
(574) 217-7584
www.corndance.com
Open daily for dinner.

The name of this restaurant has a history dating back to the Potawatomi Indians who lived in the area for 200 years. They were dependent on the land where they settled for food, shelter and clothing. Songs, legends and, surely, recipes were passed from mother to daughter as they worked in the cornfields. A good harvest was celebrated with corndances, thus the name. The restaurant draws from this history in that the majority of the food served is from local organic farms, Amish farmer markets and the owner's American Bison Ranch. Bison meatloaf, burgers, salmon, and hand-cut steaks are among the signature dishes. There are daily food and wine specials, including a three course prix fixe dinner on Wednesdays.

COURT STREET CAFE

39 East Court Street
Franklin, IN 46131
(317) 739-0208
www.courtstcafe.com
Open Monday-Friday for breakfast, lunch & dinner; Saturday for breakfast & lunch. Closed Sunday.

Facing the well-preserved Franklin County courthouse, the cafe offers some interesting twists of familiar foods. "Panfrunolas" (stuffed pancakes) are an option for breakfast, along with a slider size mini-egg sandwich. In addition to a red, white and blue slaw, salads include a berry avocado chicken and a stuffed tomato plate. There are platters, flatbreads, special sandwiches and burgers. Dessert choices include a salted caramel, bacon and strawberry flatbread in a shareable size.

COVERED BRIDGE RESTAURANT

5787 North Main Street
Eugene, IN 47928
(765) 492-7376
Open daily for breakfast, lunch & dinner.

Located on the Big Vermillion River, you can look out the back windows of the restaurant and view the second longest single span covered bridge in Indiana. Originally a grocery store and gas station before extensive renovations, it now has the atmosphere of an old country store with framed historical photos covering the walls, mementos of the town history, and 450 license plates from all 50 states and around the world. The menu is simply "good ol' Indiana food" served familystyle, and catfish is the specialty, along with many varieties of homemade pies—coconut cream is a favorite. No alcohol is served.

CRYSTAL & JULES

709 West Main Street
Madison, IN 47250
(812) 274-1077
www.crystalandjules.com
Open Tuesday-Saturday for dinner. Closed Sunday & Monday.

Named for his wife, Crystal, and mother, Julie, the owner first experienced the restaurant business by working at McDonald's at the age of fourteen. There, he claimed to have learned how to make people happy. What a gift! He went on to receive his culinary education at well-known schools. Today, whether talking about Madison restaurants, steaks or desserts, the label "the best" is often attached to Crystal & Jules. Pasta is hand-made and hand rolled in house and is incorporated into tasty combinations, many with seafood. There is steak, duck, chicken and pork that can be paired with complementary wines. Creme brûlée is the most popular dessert.

DAPPER PIG

1112 Parrett Street
Evansville, IN 47713
(812) 401-3333
www.thedapperpigevansville.com
Open Monday-Saturday for dinner. Saturday & Sunday for brunch.

The name Dapper Pig does not bring to mind a restaurant located in an historic district (Haynies Corner Arts) serving artisan food and drink. However, those are the facts about this very special restaurant recommended not only by Evansville residents but also by a person in the Washington, DC airport. The menu changes weekly and is explained as American food prepared with Japanese and French influence. Ingredients are locally sourced. There is an on-site bakery that offers items to take out. Specialty drinks are also popular with names like "2 Left Feet" and "Long Tall Sally."

DAS DUTCHMAN ESSENHAUS

240 U.S. 20
Middlebury, IN 46540
(574) 825-9471; (800) 455-9471
www.essenhaus.com
Open Monday-Saturday for breakfast, lunch & dinner. Closed Sunday.

Located in the heart of Amish country, you will find this restaurant and the surrounding village to be a pleasant surprise. Depending on your appetite, you can choose either a la carte or family-style meals with generous helpings made from scratch. Family-style dinners are all-you-can-eat salad and broasted chicken, plus a choice of roast beef, ham or baked steak. Amish dressing, mashed potatoes, corn, and homemade noodles are also included. Your meal is not complete without the homemade bread and apple butter, plus a variety of delectable desserts. The on-site bakery sells treats to take home.

DAWSON'S ON MAIN

1464 Main Street
Speedway, IN 46224
(317) 247-7000
www.dawsonsonmain.com
Open daily for lunch & dinner.

The menu encourages diners to "race on in" and yes, this delightful restaurant sits on a corner just one block from the Indianapolis Motor Speedway. There is a friendly neighborhood atmosphere with umbrellas over tables outside and an inviting, brick-walled, booth-lined dining room inside. The lunch fare features appetizers, salads, soups, sandwiches and entrées. The "D" on the menu designates house specialties. For dinner, there is an outstanding selection of steak and seafood entrées plus smoked baby back ribs, a peppercorn crusted pork loin, and Creole chicken.

DELICIA

5215 North College Avenue
Indianapolis, IN 46220
(317) 925-0677
www.deliciaindy.com
Open Monday-Saturday for dinner; Sunday for brunch & dinner.

Enter to the sound of Latin American music playing in the background. The lights are low and the atmosphere is invitingly contemporary: high table seats around the bar and pillow-backed booth seating. The food is "New Latin Cuisine" where flavors have been carefully blended to present the palate with a not too hot, just right taste. Consider soup as a starter, which has been described as comparable to one served in a South American home. Fish, beef and pork entrées are also enthusiastically described by knowlegeable servers.

DeLULLO'S TRATTORIA
230 West Jackson Street
Cicero, IN 46034
(765) 292-2000
www.delullositalian.com
Open Tuesday-Saturday for dinner. Closed Sunday & Monday.

When you decide to eat at DeLullo's, be sure to check the website beforehand to see what specials are posted. The chef prepares whatever sounds good to her that day, considering the season and what is available from local producers. Your entrée choices could be pizza, pasta or an Italian specialty. All are enthusiastically and attractively presented in this street-side bungalow where porch seating is available.

DILEGGE'S RESTAURANT
607 North Main Street
Evansville, IN 47711
(812) 428-3004
www.dilegges.com
Open Monday-Friday for lunch & dinner; Saturday for dinner. Closed Sunday.

With ancestors from Italy, this family-owned restaurant guarantees superb Italian cuisine, specializing in all homemade sauces and desserts from original family recipes. The menu also includes a nice selection of chicken, beef, seafood, veal and pasta dishes. Surrounded by many beautiful plants and photos of flowers, you will enjoy dining in this casual, relaxed atmosphere.

DISH RESTAURANT
3907 North Calumet Avenue, #203
Valparaiso, IN 46383
(219) 465-9221
www.dishrestaurant.net
Open Monday-Friday for lunch & dinner; Saturday for dinner. Closed Sunday.

Dishes hang from the walls and ceiling in this friendly, fine dining establishment. The creative menu changes every three months, featuring main courses and comfort foods for dinner. You should hope that the gorgonzola potato chips, oven roasted beet salad, and sesame chicken breast appear on the menu, along with lots of other delicious entrées and specials. In addition to salads and sandwiches, the lunch menu includes many dinner and pasta choices with some wonderful additions like baked macaroni and cheese with ham. There is also a full-service bar.

DOC PIERCE'S

120 N. Main Street
Mishawaka, IN 46544
(574) 255-7737
www.docpiercesrestaurant.com
Open Monday-Saturday for lunch & dinner; Sunday for dinner.

An historic downtown institution, this neighborhood restaurant has been in operation since 1976. The story of Doc Pierce, a traveling medicine man at the turn of the century, is quite unique, and the original advertisement for his "golden medical discovery" is still on the side of the building. The interior is dark but cozy with lighting provided by Tiffany-style hanging lamps and antique stained glass windows. The specialties are steaks and burgers, but you will also find plenty of other options to suit your tastes. Diners rave about the French onion soup and homemade onion rings. Their signature "Golden Discovery" cocktail is just what the doctor ordered.

DON QUIJOTE RESTAURANTE

119 East Lincolnway
Valparaiso, IN 46383
(219) 462-7976
www.donquijotevalpo.com
Open Monday-Saturday for lunch & dinner. Closed Sunday.

Advertised as the first Spanish restaurant in Indiana, the chef/owners introduce patrons to authentic Spanish cooking. The food is carefully prepared from natural ingredients emphasizing classic regional cuisines of Spain, which the chef clearly states "are not fast food." About thirty choices of tapas (appetizers) are offered, followed by sopas (gazpacho or soup of the day) and four varieties of ensalada (salad). Then, get ready for the comidas (dinners). A specialty of the house is paella, either Marinera or Valenciana. Other popular choices are marinated grilled pork loin with roasted red peppers, roasted lamb stuffed with green olives, and Trucha a la Navarra (trout). Finish your meal with one of the homemade desserts, such as the famous chocolate hazelnut cake. All of these tempting selections can be enjoyed in surroundings that look and feel like a Spanish café.

DOWNTOWN DINER

253 North Columbia Street
Frankfort, IN 46041
(765) 659-1370
Open daily for breakfast & lunch.

Just a block off Main Street, you will find the Downtown Diner with a parking lot overflowing with cars. Whether you are looking for "Lunch for breakfast or breakfast for lunch," the Diner claims, "we have you covered." Instead of omelets, scrambles or skillets, you might select French toast made with one of three different breads. Favorites include the Boxcar Breakfast Decker and the Ham Stack. Among the lunch specials is a Chicken Waffle sandwich and a Pork Express sandwich. Hamburgers are made with fresh, never frozen, Angus beef.

DUKE'S Indy

2352 South West Street
Indianapolis, IN 4622
(317) 643-6403
www.dukesindy.com
Open Monday-Friday for lunch & dinner; Saturday for dinner. Closed Sunday.

The entrance to Duke's is still through the old Ice House door, but the dining experience has a new twist. The specialty rotates daily with a different meat cooked in the outside "kitchen" each day. One customer said, "I've had some good brisket but THIS was the best!" Besides the special, the lunch menu has a limited number of items, insuring your meal is prepared with the freshest quality products available. At 5:00 pm, the fried chicken comes out and, along with three sides, is the one and only dinner entrée. On most Friday and Saturday nights, live entertainment is an additional treat—call ahead to check the schedule.

EDWARDS DRIVE-IN

2126 South Sherman Drive
Indianapolis, IN 46203
(317) 786-1638
www.edwardsdrivein.com
Open daily for lunch & dinner.

A local institution since 1957 and now nationally acclaimed, Edwards has preserved the atmosphere of the '50s with formica-topped tables and a working jukebox. Old car memorabilia decorates the walls, and a car show is held annually in the parking lot. Of course, handmade "larger than the bun" tenderloins, hand-dipped onion rings, hot dogs, and root beer floats are on the menu. If you prefer the old-fashioned curbside service, a waitress will come out to take your order.

EGGSHELL BISTRO

51 West City Center Drive
Carmel, IN 46032
(317) 660-1616
www.eggshellbistro.com
Open Wednesday-Sunday for brunch. Closed Monday & Tuesday.

The dictionary defines "bistro" as a small, modest European-style restaurant or cafe and the Eggshell is just that. One customer described the decor as "funky." Each little table has a different chair. Old hats, musical instruments, thought-provoking pictures and signs throughout add to the cheerful atmosphere. Meantime, jazz is playing in the background. The brunch menu is explained as global recipes creatively twisted; therefore, it is difficult to describe what an item like shakshuka really is. In addition to the unfamiliar, there are tasty items like an artichoke tart or sweet potato hash. Four Barrel coffee and Serendipitea are available. The bistro is located on the north side of the Carmel City Center, and seating provides opportunities to watch the passersby.

ERIKA'S PLACE
40 West Jackson Street
Cicero, IN 46034
(317) 984-9303
Open Monday-Saturday for breakfast, lunch & dinner; Sunday for breakfast & lunch.

If you are looking for a down home country breakfast, Erika's is the place to go. Biscuits and gravy, chipped beef, corned beef hash, and fried bologna are just a few of the many choices. The "2x4" with two slices of French toast and two pancakes is offered, as well as a half order of each. Signature items for lunch include a Big Manhattan, Mexi Spud, Classic Club, and taco and cobb salads. In addition to the usual sides, there are fried pickle chips, mandarin oranges, and pineapple. Erika's has a friendly, "everyone knows each other" atmosphere.

ERTEL CELLARS WINERY
3794 East County Road 1100 North
Batesville, IN 47006
(812) 933-1500
www.ertelcellarswinery.com
Open Wednesday-Sunday for lunch & dinner. Closed Monday & Tuesday.

Selling grapes to local wineries was the first undertaking of the Ertel family. In 2006, they opened their own winery and restaurant on 200 acres near Batesville. Atop a hill sits a chateau-style building with a tasting bar, lounge, restaurant, wine market and wine-making facility inside. You can eat under the wooden rafters or outdoors in good weather. Either way, the grapevines and rolling terrain provide a peaceful view. Though wine is the focus, the food menu offers many options for lunch and dinner, including sandwiches, salads, pastas, seafood, chicken, pork and beef.

EVERGREEN EATERY
530 Main Street
Rochester, IN 46975
(574) 223-3837
www.evergreeneatery.com
Open Tuesday & Wednesday for lunch & dinner;
Thursday-Saturday for breakfast, lunch & dinner; Sunday for breakfast & lunch.

With its commanding artwork, high ceilings, brick walls and clever appointments, this renovated local town eatery has maintained its inviting atmosphere. In fact, the Evergreen's mantra reads, "We believe a restaurant is more than a place to eat. It is where conversations start; friends and family laugh and share; it is where a community begins. So we invite you to sit, relax and enjoy." Years ago, kids stopped to eat at the Evergreen on the way to school. Today, what was once a cafe advertises casual fine dining where a shrimp bruschetta omelet highlights the standard breakfast fare, and sandwiches with delicious sides are offered for lunch. The fresh fish is superb but there's steak and pasta, too. Desserts are made in house from scratch.

EVIL CZECH BREWERY

3703 North Main Street
Mishawaka, IN 46545
(574) 855-3070
www.evilczechbrewery.com
Open daily for lunch & dinner.

"Life is too short to drink bad beer, but there's always time for Evil Beer!" Whether you are looking for handcrafted brews to enjoy with your meal or just a place to eat, the Evil Czech has a lot to offer. Public Plates & Snacks include pork belly corn dogs and green bean fries. Salads come in pizza crust bowls. There are tacos, sandwiches, gourmet burgers (bison, beef, chicken) and woodstone pizzas. The menu also includes several mac & cheese options and house specialties like ribs and goulash. On weekdays, Lightnin' Lunch is a way to taste it all. It is a small plate buffet with bite sizes of regular menu items.

EXCHANGE PUB & KITCHEN

118 West Main Street
New Albany, IN 47150
(812) 948-6501
www.exchangeforfood.com
Open Monday-Saturday for lunch & dinner. Closed Sunday.

The Exchange is an architectural wonder, located across the street from the New Albany Riverfront Amphitheater. It is hard to believe that the upscale restaurant of today was, in 1875, a horse livery and stable, followed by a poultry company and then a tire warehouse. A 20-foot ceiling supported by exposed steel beams looms over the booths and tables of the restaurant with a commanding stairway at one end. There is also an open air bar with outside seating. The architecture is great, but the food and drink is why you want to visit. Recommended menu items are the blueberry brie grilled cheese and the sweet chili salmon bowl. For dinner there are pork chops, salmon and a New Albany Hot Brown.

FARMbloomington

108 East Kirkwood
Bloomington, IN 47408
(812) 323-0002
www.farm-bloomington.com

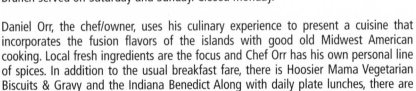

Open Tuesday-Friday for breakfast & lunch; Saturday for dinner.
Brunch served on Saturday and Sunday. Closed Monday.

Daniel Orr, the chef/owner, uses his culinary experience to present a cuisine that incorporates the fusion flavors of the islands with good old Midwest American cooking. Local fresh ingredients are the focus and Chef Orr has his own personal line of spices. In addition to the usual breakfast fare, there is Hoosier Mama Vegetarian Biscuits & Gravy and the Indiana Benedict Along with daily plate lunches, there are FARMwiches, midwest tacos and woodstone pizzas. An upstairs bar and a downstairs Root Cellar both provide a fun alternative place to drink and dine.

FARMHOUSE CAFÉ & TEA ROOM

5171 Beanblossom Road
Nineveh, IN 46164
(812) 988-2004
www.farmhousecafeandtearoom.com
Open daily for lunch; Tuesday-Saturday for dinner.

How nice it is to take a drive to Brown County and have a special meal. Seating is available in this renovated 1800s farmhouse or, in good weather, on the porch or patio. Located midst a flower and plant nursery, the area is beautifully landscaped. The menu is seasonal with emphasis on garden fresh ingredients. For lunch there are unique sandwiches like Cool as a Cucumber and an asparagus and orange salad. Dinner choices include the Farmhouse steak and grilled Atlantic salmon. Desserts are delicious and the fall menu offers persimmon pudding, an Indiana favorite.

FARMHOUSE RESTAURANT at Fair Oaks Farms

856 North 600 East
Fair Oaks, IN 47943
(877) 536-1193
www.fofarms.com
Open daily for lunch & dinner.

A visit to Fair Oaks Farms is an adventure for the entire family. It houses one of the largest working dairies in the country, a birthing farm, cheese factory, market, bakery, and this family sit-down restaurant. With its mission to offer unparalleled hospitality, the Farmhouse staff welcomes you as guests in their home. Wood floors, beamed ceilings with large chandeliers, and a huge stone hearth fireplace create a warm and inviting atmosphere. Food is prepared in the glass-enclosed kitchen overlooking the main dining room. Menu items are familiar, but freshly made from ingredients that are grown and harvested at Fair Oaks and other farms located within the region.

FOXGARDIN KITCHEN & ALE

215 South Main Street
Fortville, IN 46040
(317) 485-4085
www.foxgardin.com
Open daily for lunch & dinner.

Dining at the FoxGardin provides a great reason to go to Fortville, a small town close to Indianapolis but seemingly "out in the country." Walking up and down Main Street fills you with nostalgia: quaint shops, ice cream, saddlery, and an old fire house. Daily specials are listed on a chalkboard over the bar. Along with items like Bang Mi and Lobster BLT, there are "seasonal American" entrees that have interesting twists. Advertised as a "gastropub," this well describes the FoxGardin.

FRIENDLY TAVERN

290 South Main Street
Zionsville, IN 46077
(317) 873-5772
www.friendlytavernzionsville.com
Open Monday-Saturday for lunch & dinner. Closed Sunday.

The statement on the menu, "You are a stranger here but once," well describes the name and atmosphere of the Friendly Tavern. The building dates back over 100 years and a sign lets you know that it wasn't always a restaurant: "Zionsville Carriage and Wagon Works, 1875." However, the Friendly has provided a gathering place serving food and drink to people in the area for over 60 years. Tenderloins, burgers, and reuben sandwiches are popular, along with Friendly's famous wings and sauces. Steaks, chicken, pork chops and fish are available for dinner and there is a prime rib special on Thursday through Saturday nights "while supplies last."

FRONT PORCH STEAK HOUSE

118 North Canal Street
Worthington, IN 47471
(812) 875-2306
Open Sunday & Tuesday for breakfast & lunch;
Wednesday-Saturday for breakfast, lunch & dinner. Closed Monday.
CASH AND CHECKS ONLY.

Originally an old filling station, the owners have created a warm and inviting atmosphere, specializing in home-cooked meals and homemade pies. The interior was divided into sections for dining areas, cathedral ceilings added, and accent shelves installed to display a collection of crockery and antiques. Benches on the front porch invite you to sit and relax before or after your meal. They are known for excellent steaks, catfish, and spaghetti with homemade sauce, but people come from all over for the prime rib on Friday and Saturday and the popular pan-fried chicken on Sunday. There is also a variety of lunch specials and the traditional breakfast fare.

GAITHER CAFÉ at Gaither Family Resources

1617 South Park Avenue (State Road 9 South)
Alexandria, IN 46001
(765) 724-8405 or (800) 520-4664
www.gaitherfamilyresources.com
Open Monday-Saturday for breakfast, lunch & dinner. Closed Sunday.

The cafe is just a small part of the Gaither complex, so you should plan to spend a few hours there to see and enjoy all they have to offer. This is a "pure and simple restaurant" that serves breakfast, lunch and dinner. The menu is extensive, filled with soups, salads, sandwiches, pastas, and popular plates. Special coffee drinks and mouthwatering homemade desserts are an added treat. The Gaithers are well-known in the gospel music circle and people come from all over to share their music. Committed to "serving needs from birth to death," the facility is divided into sections: Comfort Area, Classics, Home Care, Less Stress, and Loving Graces. There are unique gifts, books, home and garden accessories, jewelry, toys, and a huge display of Christmas decorations sprinkled throughout.

GALO'S ITALIAN GRILL
107 Garwood Road
Richmond, IN 47374
(765) 973-9000
www.galositalian.com
Open daily for lunch & dinner.

You walk into a circular restaurant with columns, statues and wall coverings that all suggest a setting in Italy. The staff is extremely friendly, and the menu should satisfy various appetites. The antipasti salad is generous in size and is accompanied by the best toasted flatbread. In addition to the special pasta entrées, there are poultry, meat and seafood choices. Wood-fired pizzas are "hand-stretched" and come with regular or whole wheat crust. Gluten-free pasta is available.

GAMBA RISTORANTE
455 East 84th Drive
Merrillville, IN 46140
(219) 736-5000
www.gambaristorante.com
Open Monday-Friday for lunch & dinner; Saturday for dinner. Closed Sunday.

A favorite stop when traveling to or from Chicago, Gamba's offers unique and wonderful northern Italian food. As you enter the restaurant, circular patterns catch your eye: the globe chandeliers, the alcoves, the glasses, and the rooms. While the atmosphere is upscale, it is as comfortable and inviting as their slogan suggests: "Where Family Becomes Family." The seasonal menu offers five courses plus dessert. Dishes are listed with their Italian names and then described in mouthwatering terms. The lunch menu is not simply smaller portions of items on the dinner menu; it includes additional choices in each of the five courses. You can eat lunch on your way to Chicago and dinner on your way home and have completely different taste experiences.

GARCIA'S MEXICAN RESTAURANT
3932 25th Street
Columbus, IN 47203
(812) 376-0783
Open Tuesday-Thursday for lunch; Friday for lunch & dinner.
Closed Saturday-Monday. Closed January-March.
CASH ONLY ESTABLISHMENT.

This family-owned restaurant is tucked away in back of a small shopping center. As you step inside, you will immediately notice the colorful and sparkling interior that creates a very inviting atmosphere. Comfortable seating is provided in alcoves of white stucco. Chips are served with both a sweet and hot sauce, a combination of flavors that tastefully complement each other. The menu is very straightforward with taco, enchilada and tostada combinations, along with burritos, chimichangas and chile relleno. The guacamole is excellent.

GEORGE'S NEIGHBORHOOD GRILL
6935 Lake Plaza
Indianapolis, IN 46220
(317) 577-1600
www.georgesneighborhoodgrill.com
Open daily for lunch & dinner.

As residents of the area, the owners wanted neighbors to feel at home while dining at their establishment. George's has accomplished that and more, becoming a popular gathering spot for nearby neighbors and area residents. Whether you eat in the sports bar or the family room, you will see a broad cross-section of people surrounded by TVs projecting the daily news and sports events. The menu has something for everyone. Appetizers include many choices like wings, waffle fries and little sliders. Salad favorites are the Black Forest with black cherry vinaigrette dressing and the grilled chicken and spinach with honey mustard dressing. Each day there are specials but you can always get a filet, fish, chicken or pasta dish. Pizzas and sandwiches are also available. Gluten-free items are highlighted. If you carry out, curbside pick-up is an option.

GERST BAVARIAN HAUS
2100 West Franklin Street
Evansville, IN 47712
(812) 424-1420
www.gersthausevansville.com
Open daily for lunch & dinner.

The Gerst Brewing Company opened in Nashville, Tennessee, in 1890 and flourished for many years, winning awards for its beers. When the brewery closed, a restaurant evolved but closed again when the Tennessee Titans football stadium was constructed on the site. The owners relocated to Evansville and took over the space of the Heldt and Voelker hardware store, a building that was considered to be a prime example of turn of the century architecture. The windows still carry the hardware store advertisements, but inside you feel like you are in a German beer hall, complete with high ceilings, red and white checked tablecloths, flags and music. American food items are on the menu, but the main focus is German: potato pancakes, sauerkraut, bratwurst, knackwurst, schnitzels, sauerbraten, goulash, and the world famous Gerst Kasseler Rippchen (one-pound smoked pork chop). There are draft and bottled beers from over 25 countries available.

GIOVANNI'S

603 Ridge Road
Munster, IN 46321
(219) 836-6220
www.giosmunster.com
Open Monday-Friday for lunch & dinner; Saturday for dinner. Closed Sunday.

Procopio LoDuca immigrated to the United States as a young boy and achieved his dream of opening a small pizza restaurant at this location in 1966. Later, he enlarged and remodeled to become the Giovanni's of today, still family owned and operated. One specialty is the Nothing BeatZZA Pizza, but the chef's crab cakes, hand-made ravioli, veal rollatini, and grilled pork medallions are mouthwatering alternatives. You must also consider the daily specials, decided upon early in the morning based on the best available ingredients in the market that day. Customer service is of utmost importance to the staff and is evident when you dine here.

GOOD MORNING MAMA'S CAFÉ

1001 East 54th Street
Indianapolis, IN 46220
(317) 255-3800
www.goodmorningmamas.com
Open Tuesday-Sunday for breakfast & lunch. Closed Monday.

You will take a step back to the '40s when you enter this old filling station, transformed into a delightful daytime restaurant. A juke box, Betty Boop, formica table tops and vinyl chairs add to the colorful atmosphere that gets your day started right. Along with omelets, French toast and pancakes, breakfast specialties include Hawaiian Loco Mocos and Elvis' favorite (a surprise). For lunch, there are salads, soups, paninis, plus hot and cold sandwiches. Champagne mimosas, beer and wine are also available.

GOOSE THE MARKET

2503 North Delaware Street
Indianapolis, IN 46205
(317) 924-4944
www.goosethemarket.com
Open Monday-Saturday for lunch & dinner. Closed Sunday.

As the name implies, Goose is a market, albeit a very special market, catering to those who seek unique ingredients found in tasty recipes. Local Indiana producers provide many of the items for sale: seasonal vegetables, honey, meat, cheese, gelati and baked goods. The products foreign to Indiana growers are also of the best quality: Fair Trade coffee, Italian and Spanish olive oils, wines, beers and many other items. A part of stocking good food is offering the customer the opportunity to taste it, and the Goose accomplishes this through the sale of soups, sandwiches, rolls and cookies. Rotating choices are advertised on the website. There is also a special place downstairs called Enoteca where there are communal tables for wine or beer tasting and a small plate menu that includes cheese and charcuterie boards.

GOSPEL BIRD

207 East Main Street
New Albany, IN 47150
(812) 725-1054
www.orderthebird.com
Open Tuesday-Saturday for lunch & dinner. Sunday for brunch. Closed Monday.

The name and the riverside location grab your attention. Then, the renovated space with a barroom and dining room draws you in: brick walls, wooden ceiling fans, door dividers, salvaged tin ceiling tiles on a wall and, of course, a huge rooster picture. The menu advertises southern comfort food with a New American flair, and it is constantly changing. The names are catchy like Idgie & Ruth fried green tomatoes and a "mop sauce" brisket sandwich with collard greens and spicy pickles. The dinner menu might feature shrimp and grits, Nashville fish, thunder thighs or Korean smoked brisket. No matter what you choose, every bite has a combination of delightful flavors.

GRAINS & GRILL

407 West Washington Street
Fairmount, IN 46928
(765) 380-0137
www.grainsandgrill.com
Open Monday-Saturday for dinner. Closed Sunday.

Along with Bad Dad's Brewery, the restaurant is located in an old John Deere establishment. There's a factory feel to the structure with exposed vents and lights made out of funnels. Comfort foods like burgers, pork tenderloins and mac and cheese are available, but the specialties are steaks and seafood. The in-house brewery offers many special brews. Grains & Grill is a good place to eat after exploring the attractions of Fairmount. The actor James Dean was a Fairmount resident and probably would have enjoyed eating here.

GRAY BROTHERS CAFETERIA

555 South Indiana Street
Mooresville, IN 46158
(317) 831-7234
www.graybroscafe.com
Open daily for lunch & dinner.

Dating back to 1944, three generations of Grays have upheld the high quality of their cafeteria. The tradition continues today with a promise that there will always be a Gray in charge. Fortunately, the first item to be selected is your dessert. It would be a crime to leave Gray's without sampling the fresh strawberry or lemon meringue pie. Of course, there's a wonderful selection of other homemade pies, cakes and desserts as well. Each day's entrées are listed on the website and include chicken, fish, pork and beef prepared in special ways. Salad, vegetables and rolls are offered to accompany your meal. Portions are generous, and you'll be happy you committed to the dessert first.

GRIGGSBY'S STATION

101 West Main Street
Greenfield, IN 46140
(317) 477-7217
www.griggsbysstation.com
Open Monday-Saturday for dinner. Closed Sunday.

Located on the square in Greenfield, the restaurant is named after a poem by local poet James Whitcomb Riley. Griggsby's is committed to using locally sourced ingredients and promises that all the protein on their menu comes from "pasture to pub." The restaurant has partnered with Tyner Pond Farm to offer the most nutritious products. Deviled eggs and buffalo chicken dip are on the appetizer list. Follow the starter with steaks, pork chops, sandwiches or a variety of burgers. As the owners state, "It's all about what is sustainable, fresh, and in season."

HALF MOON RESTAURANT & BREWERY

4051 South LaFountain Street
Kokomo, IN 46902
(765) 455-2739
www.halfmoonbrewery.com
Open daily for lunch & dinner.

Located on U.S. Highway 31 South, the Half Moon can be mistaken for one of the many chain restaurants in the area, but that is not the case. This locally owned restaurant and brewery has many surprises. The baked brewer rolls and special butters whet the appetite. There are sandwiches, burgers, pasta, and the normal main course choices; however, the key to their tastiness is in the preparation. The smokehouse entrées of ribs, brisket, and chicken are seasoned with homemade dry rubs and sauces. Other specialty items like Jack Daniel's Sirloin and Porter Glazed Chutney Chops attest to the uniqueness of the menu. The brewery is housed in the building and fresh brews can be purchased.

HAUB HOUSE

101 East Haub Street
Haubstadt, IN 47639
(812) 768-6462; (800) 654-1158
www.haubhouse.com
Open Monday-Saturday for dinner. Closed Sunday.

This former warehouse built in the early 1900s has been remodeled into a charming southern colonial straight out of Williamsburg. Decorated with wood paneling and large chandeliers, each dining room carries out the colonial theme. You can choose to dine in the Manor Room or the Kensington Room. There are over 50 entrées on the menu, including prime beef and fresh seafood. Reservations are recommended on weekends.

HEDGE ROW

350 Massachusetts Avenue
Indianapolis, IN 46204
(317) 643-2750
www.hedgerowbistros.com
Open for lunch and dinner daily.

Hedge Row's promise is to offer "wood roasted real food from American farmers." As you enter the restaurant, a blackboard advertises foods sourced from the Smoking Goose, Fischer Farms, Gunthrop Farms, etc., assuring quality ingredients. There are snacks, small plates and large plates, from an appetizer of Harissa honey almonds to a New York strip steak entrée. In between, there are fish lettuce wraps, grilled chicken green goddess salad, and even a char-grilled burger. Hedge Row is located on busy Mass Ave and offers complimentary parking.

HEINNIES

1743 West Lusher Avenue
Elkhart, IN 46517
(574) 522-9101
Open Monday-Friday for lunch & dinner;
Saturday for dinner. Closed Sunday.

Over 50 years ago, the location of Heinnies was carefully chosen to be close to the railroad tracks. Three generations of the DeShone family have molded the restaurant into what it is today. The "back barn" offers a seating alternative to the colorful bar area and has an old stove and a piano in the loft. Although best known for their award-winning cheeseburgers and steaks, the menu has other alternatives along with a daily special.

HENRY SOCIAL CLUB

423 Washington Street
Columbus, IN 47201
(812) 799-1371
www.henrysocialclub.com
Open Tuesday-Friday.for lunch & dinner. Dinner only on Saturday.
Closed Sunday and Monday.

Excellent food delivered by a pleasant staff is a welcomed introduction to the Henry Social Club. The open concept kitchen enables diners seated closeby to see the meals in varying stages of preparation. If lucky, seats at the counter might be available. Deviled eggs and bacon wrapped dates are tasty starters. In addition to pizza and pasta offerings, there are creatively prepared fish, chicken and beef entrées.Homemade bread and Sophia's butterscotch pudding enhance the meal and make dining in downtown Columbus a real treat.

HERITAGE TRAIL CAFE AND COFFEE ROASTER

206 North Sale Street
Ellettsville, IN 47429
(812) 935-5335
www.heritagetrailcafeandcoffeeroaster.com
Open Monday-Saturday for breakfast & lunch. Closed Sunday.

The in-house roasted coffee, black or fancy, draws you in BUT there are tasty reasons to have a bite to eat. Breakfast sandwiches and casseroles contain a cayenne candied bacon that is delicious. For lunch, there are homemade soups and salads plus daily specials; look for the "Muddy Fork." Fresh baked pastries are enticing and there are yummy cookies to go. Ellettsville is an old Indiana town where Heritage Trail is on the main street.

HESTON SUPPER CLUB

2003 E 1000 N
LaPorte, IN 46350
(219) 778-2938
www.hestonsupperclub.com
Open daily for dinner.

If you are traveling on I-94 and feeling hungry, turn off at Exit One (New Buffalo). As you wander down a Galena Township country road, you will come to the town of Heston. What used to be a combination dairy, general store and tavern in the 1940s simply became the Heston Bar. "Supper Club" was added to the name in 1982 when the current owners committed to providing a fine dining experience in a casual supper club atmosphere. Complimentary cheese and crackers await you. At the top of the dining choices is the award-winning slow-roasted prime rib with au jus and homemade horseradish sauce. Hand-cut steaks, Colorado lamb chops, Canadian walleye, and lake perch are also on the menu. All meals include homemade soup, salad and a side dish.

HICKORY HILLS BARBECUE

16021 North US Highway 31
Edinburgh, IN 46124
(812) 526-5280
Open Tuesday-Saturday for lunch & dinner. Closed Sunday & Monday.

A day at the Edinburgh Outlet Mall should include a stop at Hickory Hills Barbecue, either to enjoy a meal or to carry one home. Eating space is limited in this no-frills restaurant, but there is a small area for dining outside or in the garage. Smoked chicken, pork and beef brisket are the choices for sandwiches. On Friday and Saturday, ribs and rib tips are additional options. The daily specials include gumbo on Tuesday and hot sausage on Thursday. Homemade key lime pie is available for dessert, the perfect complement to the barbecue flavors.

HILLTOP INN
1100 Harmony Way
Evansville, IN 47720
(812) 422-1757
Open Monday-Saturday for lunch & dinner. Closed Sunday.

Built in 1839, this restaurant was originally an old saloon and stagecoach stop. Located high on a hill just two miles from the Ohio River, it was a popular stop for weary travelers. It has maintained a very rustic, country atmosphere and features an over 70-year-old back bar. Hilltop offers your basic down home country cookin'–fried chicken, steaks and fiddlers–but if you are the more adventuresome type, you must try the brain sandwich, an unusual but popular menu item.

HILLTOP RESTAURANT
2434 N. U.S. 231
Spencer, IN 47460
(812) 829-3891
Open Wednesday-Friday for dinner; Saturday & Sunday for lunch & dinner.
Closed Monday & Tuesday.

Situated on a hilltop in Southern Indiana's "Sweet Owen" County, this restaurant has been a popular dining spot for many years. Originally known as the Skyland Lodge, it boasted the reputation for fine family dining, a tradition it upholds today. The words over the fireplace tell the story: "Thru our doors come the finest people in the land, our friends, you folk." The specialties are Spencer steak and fried chicken, which are accompanied by a feast: salad, tomato juice, pickled beets, vegetable sticks, mashed potatoes, green beans, corn and homemade rolls with orange marmalade. If that isn't enough, treat yourself to Mississippi Mud Cake or persimmon pudding for dessert.

HINO OISHI
10491 Walnut Creek Drive
Carmel, IN 46032
(317) 228-0888
www.hinooishi.com
Open daily for lunch & dinner.

No matter what you order, the food comes out looking and tasting fresh and crisp and as one customer described it, "Yummy." Each artfully presented entrée is a treat to the eye. You may choose to sit at a community table and have an entertaining meal presentation or in the comfortable and inviting bar area. A blackboard lists the daily specials. In addition to the sushi menu, the regular offerings are well-described as "hibachi" land, sea, or combination, and "youshoku" Japanese-Western cuisine. Appetizers, salads, Bento boxes, teriyaki and vegetarian choices are available. They promise the food is "always oishi" (delicious).

HISTORIC STEER-IN

5130 East 10th Street
Indianapolis, IN 46219
(317) 356-0996
www.steerin.net
Open daily for breakfast & lunch; Tuesday-Sunday for dinner.

Originally the Northway Drive-In, it became Harold's Steer-In in 1964, a popular week-end spot to cruise and dine curbside. Harold added to the building in 1985, providing a place for families to come in and "feed their grumbling stomachs." Waffles, biscuits and gravy, and omelettes accompanied by Harold's fried potatoes are all good ways to start the day. Sandwich specialties are the twin burger and the tenderloin. Harold's recipe for cole slaw and coconut cream pie have not been lost. The pizza dough is made in the kitchen and is special, too. Wine, beer and micro beers are available.

HOBNOB CORNER

17 West Main Street
Nashville, IN 47448
(812) 988-4114
www.hobnobcornerrestaurant.com
Open Wednesday-Monday for breakfast, lunch & dinner;
Tuesday for breakfast & lunch.

Built in 1873 as a dry goods/grocery store, pictures and antique relics scattered throughout tell the history of the Hobnob establishment and of Nashville. Today, the restaurant offers recipes from the past like biscuits and gravy and loggers hash for breakfast, and pot roast or liver and onions for lunch. Since the last "Dining Secrets" publication, Hobnob has added an After-Five Menu, which includes wine. Whether dining on pork tenderloin, duck breast, bistro tender or a seasonal special, it is well worth Hobnobbing!

HOLLYHOCK HILL

8110 North College Avenue
Indianapolis, IN 46240
(317) 251-2294
www.hollyhockhill.com
Open Tuesday-Saturday for dinner;
Sunday for lunch & dinner. Closed Monday.

In 1928, the original owners began serving dinners at their country cottage on Indy's north side. Because of the many beautiful hollyhocks on the premises, it soon became known as Hollyhock Hill. One of a few family-style restaurants still in existence, Hollyhock stands out from others not only for the excellent food but for its more formal ambiance. Floral curtains and fresh flowers on the tables fill the light and airy dining rooms. Steaks and shrimp are on the menu, but the fried chicken is the most popular, accompanied by a feast of vegetables, salad with their famous sweet-sour dressing, homemade pickled beets, apple butter and homemade biscuits. Ice cream with a choice of toppings completes this memorable dining experience.

HOMESTEAD

36 South Ohio Street
Remington, IN 47977
(219) 261-2138
www.homesteadbuttery.com
Open Monday-Saturday for breakfast & lunch. Closed Sunday.

It isn't clear upon entering the restaurant if you are in grandma's kitchen or the local country store. Either way, the homey atmosphere is comfortable and the aromas make you hungry. Assemble your own salad or order a sandwich to be delivered to your table. The Homestead Stack is an outstanding assortment of sandwich makings. The prepared foods for sale in the store carry out the mission of helping simplify the lives of their customers: frozen casseroles, pies, soups, jars of peaches, jellies, candies, etc. Reportedly, the bakers start making the bread at 2 am.

HONEYSUCKLE HILL BEE-STRO

6367 North Murphy Road
Brazil, IN 47834
(812) 443-3003
www.honeysucklehillbee.com
Open Friday & Saturday March-December for lunch & dinner.

What a surprise to find a "bee-stro" on top of a hill, overlooking a peaceful country lake. The name is appropriate since the restaurant is owned by a family of beekeepers, and honey is included in at least a third of the made-from-scratch recipes. Sayings like, "You are the bees knees," honeycomb fixtures, bee pictures and napkin rings decorate the inviting dining room in a little yellow house on the owners' property. Using the weekly lunch or dinner menu as a guide, guests write their own orders. For lunch, there's quiche, chicken salad with honey, a cola burger, and a "bites plate" that offers a taste of three items. Dinner could feature a peach stuffed pork chop, bacon wrapped chicken thighs, or a NY strip steak. Honey beehive cake is a great complement to your meal. Honey, beekeeping supplies and gift items are for sale in the shop upstairs.

HOUSE OF COMO

2700 South Kentucky Avenue (Highway 41 South)
Evansville, IN 47714
(812) 422-0572
Open Tuesday-Saturday for dinner. Closed Sunday & Monday.
CASH AND CHECKS ONLY.

Many consider this the best restaurant in Evansville, and comments made by the founder several years ago confirm that: "I don't need any advertising. I have all the business I can handle!" The restaurant is in an unlikely location so look for the Santa Claus over the door. As you walk inside, you will notice there are more Santa Claus figures everywhere. Little has changed since the restaurant has been in operation. The steaks, pork chops, pasta, seafood and sandwiches are all excellent, but the unusual items on the menu are the Arabian dishes. The Arabian salad in a delicately light lemon dressing arrives in a bowl and is then folded into Arabian bread. Eggplant, stuffed cabbage leaves and baked chicken Djage are also wonderful.

IARIA'S ITALIAN RESTAURANT
317 South College Avenue
Indianapolis, IN 46202
(317) 638-7706
www.iariasrestaurant.com
Open Tuesday-Friday for lunch & dinner; Saturday for dinner.
Closed Sunday & Monday.

The Iaria family came to the United States from Calabria, located at the very tip of the boot of Italy. This family-owned restaurant opened in 1933 and continues to offer wonderful Italian dishes prepared from recipes passed down through generations. Very little of the original decor has changed over the years, but the comfortable atmosphere makes it an inviting place to bring the family. The lunch and dinner menus are the same, offering meat and spinach ravioli, meatballs and Italian sausage, pizza, pastas served with a choice of sauces, plus delicious homemade garlic bread. You will also enjoy the cheesecake, cannoli, or spumoni for dessert.

ICHIBAN NOODLES SUSHI RESTAURANT
8355 Bash Street
Indianapolis, IN 46250
(317) 841-0484
Open Monday-Saturday for lunch & dinner. Closed Sunday.

On the road to the Castleton Post Office there is a little white house with a handmade sign that says "noodles." Don't be fooled by the outside. Stop in and see this small, well-organized restaurant. The sushi bar is set up at the entrance and the owner prepares the rolls and the nigiri (rice with fish on top). Bento crates are compartmentalized boxes offering an opportunity to taste a variety of food items. Donburi (a bowl of rice covered with your choice of stew) is on the menu, as are three types of noodles served in a variety of ways. Japanese beer and saki are also available.

IOZZO'S GARDEN OF ITALY
946 South Meridian Street
Indianapolis, IN 46225
(317) 974-1100
www.iozzos.com
Open Monday-Friday for lunch & dinner; Saturday & Sunday for dinner.

Iozzo's claims to be the "newest oldest" Italian restaurant in Indianapolis. In fact, the history begins in 1930 when Fred Iozzo opened the Naples Grill as the first full-service Italian restaurant in town. In 1941, at the onset of America's entry into the war, Fred got into trouble while defending the honor of one of his daughters. That event eventually closed the restaurant, but it was reopened in 2009 by one of Fred's great-granddaughters. Katie invites you to experience the traditional Italian recipes of her family. The servers are eager to match the diners' tastes with the menu offerings and often suggest trying the meatballs as an appetizer or main course. Small plates are offered mid-afternoon before the dinner hour. There is a Garden of Italy dinner for two that includes an antipasti plate, wedding soup or salad, spaghetti and meatballs or sausage, and spumoni for dessert.

IRON SKILLET

2489 West 30th Street
Indianapolis, IN 46222
(317) 923-6353
www.ironskillet.net
Open Wednesday-Saturday for dinner;
Sunday for lunch & dinner. Closed Monday & Tuesday.

The Iron Skillet was originally the clubhouse for Highland Country Club and became a restaurant in 1956. Its location on a hilltop between two public golf courses offers a lovely, peaceful view. There are several different rooms, each having a light and airy atmosphere. Family-style dining makes the Iron Skillet a great place to gather for group celebrations. Each diner chooses an entrée of chicken, shrimp, fish, or steak and then a set menu of appetizers, side dishes and homemade baking powder biscuits accompany the meals. Ice cream or sherbet with a choice of assorted toppings is also included. You leave feeling like you've been to granny's home in the country.

ITALIAN HOUSE ON PARK

219 Park Street
Westfield, IN 46074
(317) 804-5619
www.theitalianhouseonpark.com
Open Tuesday-Saturday for dinner. Closed Sunday & Monday.

Located just east of US 31, the Italian House is easily accessible off Main Street in Westfield. Tables are set in the various rooms, including the porch, of a charming old house. The cuisine is contemporary Italian with pesce, carne, scallopine and of course pasta options. Most enticing, however, are the daily specials presented with a gourmet flair. Pride is taken in the desserts of tiramasu, gelato and panne cotta. The Backyard Bar is fully enclosed and located on the outside patio where customers can dine or relax and enjoy cocktails in a comfortable seating area.

JACQUIE'S

9840 North Michigan Road
Carmel, IN 46032
(317) 875-5227
www.jacquiesgourmetcafe.com
Open Monday-Saturday for breakfast & lunch. Sunday for brunch.

Jacquie's has the look and feel of a neighborhood cafe, decorated with colorful pictures and paintings. "Help yourself" coffee pots are a nice convenience when you need a refill. The breakfast menu features some old standbys of oatmeal, smoked salmon and omelettes of the day; other items are prepared with a creative twist—the pancakes lemon ricotta and granola yogurt parfait are delicious. For lunch, among the homemade soup of the day and sandwich favorites, there are creative salads of curried chicken and a winter apple salad with champagne vinaigrette. Jacquie's also offers gourmet catering.

JANKO'S LITTLE ZAGREB

223 West 6th Street
Bloomington, IN 47404
(812) 332-0694
www.littlezagreb.com
Open Monday-Saturday for dinner. Closed Sunday.

"Janko" is "Little Johnny" and Zagreb is the capital of Croatia. The restaurant's name commemorates Janko's grandmother who, as he was growing up, repeatedly talked about how much food people ate when they worked on the farms. The interior is decorated with red and white checked tablecloths, silverware wrapped in waxed paper, and posters on the walls. As you open the menu, you are informed that "all steaks are thick." Although the steaks are a specialty and superb, there is quite a variety of other choices, including barbecued ribs with a special hot sauce, thick juicy pork chops, meatballs Bucharest, porterhouse lamb chops, Punjene stuffed pepper, and additional taste treats.

JASMINE THAI RESTAURANT

4825 East 96th Street
Indianapolis, IN 46240
(317) 848-8950
www.jasminethaiindy.com
Open daily for lunch & dinner.

Jasmine provides you with a wonderful opportunity to eat a healthy meal. The restaurant offers soups, salads, rice & noodle dishes, Thai curries, and a few traditional meals. Lunch specials are offered during the week. The satay and salad rolls are tasty appetizers. Drunken noodles (pad ki-mao) and Panang curry are flavor-filled entrées. The staff, many of whom are related to the owner, takes pride in pleasing the customers. If you have any concerns about mild, medium or hot, the servers understand and accommodate, even if the meal needs to be sent back to the kitchen.

J. FORD'S BLACK ANGUS

502 South 3rd Street
Terre Haute, IN 47807
(812) 235-5549
www.jfordsblackangus.com
Open Tuesday-Saturday for dinner. Closed Sunday & Monday.

If you are hungry for a steak from the famous Chicago Stockyards™, you can find it in Terre Haute. Jeff and Kelly Ford have taken an old restaurant, created an upscale menu, and now serve meals graciously in a small, intimate dining room with background music of the past. Lobster corn dogs and portabello fries are on the appetizer menu and an Angus wedge or roasted pears are among the salad choices. Along with the steaks, there are other enticing entrées of veal, pork belly, and seafood. The food and the hospitality make the trip worthwhile. A discriminating Dining Secrets reader called the filet "excellent."

JIALLO'S

5130 West 38th Street
Indianapolis, IN 46254
(317) 492-1603
www.jiallos.com
Open daily for lunch & dinner.

Jiallo comes to Indiana from Guinea, West Africa and introduces Hoosiers to the African/Caribbean cuisine of his ancestors. It is what can be called a "humble" restaurant on the west side of Indianapolis in an area known as the International Marketplace. The menu has familiar words like "jerk" but then there is attieke (a kind of couscous) and Tiebdjen, a national fried fish dish of Senegal. The vegetable sides are exceptional with options like fried plantains and onion tomato stir fry. Carry-out and catering services are also available.

JIMMIE'S DAIRY BAR

7065 South State Road 67
Pendleton, IN 46064
(765) 778-3800
www.jimmiesdairybar.com
Open daily for lunch & dinner.

Drive up or dine in at this retro restaurant of the 1950s. Order your favorites off a menu that is well-stocked with items famous from that era: milkshakes, chocolate sodas, slushes, floats, onion rings, fried mushrooms, and coney dogs. Or, the proclamation that the "best BBQ in Indiana is served right here" might draw you to this location. Homemade tangerine and strawberry ice cream are yummy, too.

JOCKAMO UPPER CRUST PIZZA

5646 East Washington Street
Indianapolis, IN 46219
(317) 356-6612
www.jockamopizza.com
Open daily for lunch & dinner.

Located in the historic Irvington neighborhood, Jockamo is a "no frills" pizza restaurant with a very friendly atmosphere. Paintings by local artists decorate the walls and change regularly as pieces are sold. The bar area is a great gathering spot to watch the games on big screen TVs. The pizza is the story here. They make their own sauce and crust and grind a mix of mozzarella and Parmesan cheeses daily. Fresh ingredients are purchased from local vendors to create some unique combinations, such as the Cheese Louise, Thai Chicken, Slaughterhouse Five, Shipwreck, and Potato Skin pizzas. Appetizers, salads and sandwiches are also available. Vegetarian requests are honored, too.

JOSEPH DECUIS

191 North Main Street
Roanoke, IN 46783
(260) 672-1715
www.josephdecuis.com
Open Monday-Saturday for dinner. Closed Sunday.

One of the most memorable dining experiences awaits you in this small Indiana town. The ambiance is of Old World luxury and comfort with each room offering a different venue. Club Creole is a formal dining room and bar located in the historic Roanoke State Bank building. Two original bank vaults house the walk-in cigar humidor and nationally-acclaimed wine cellar. Café Creole is the entrance dining room and features the exhibition kitchen where you can watch the culinary artists at work. A Victorian conservatory offers dining in tropical elegance, and an outdoor New Orleans-style courtyard is surrounded by beautifully landscaped gardens. The cuisine is gourmet dining in the Creole tradition, an imaginative blend of classical cooking, unique ingredients, and artful presentation. The dinner menu changes weekly to feature the finest and freshest ingredients and allows for the chef's creativity. A typical dinner selection might include a Caribbean seafood cocktail appetizer, hoisin duck salad, and an entrée of pan sautéed Dover sole or a fresh herb-crusted rack of lamb. Be sure to look at the Tim Johnson oil paintings and sculptures when you visit.

Do you have some extra time on your hands after visiting one of the restaurants?

Are you looking for somewhere to stop to satisfy your sweet tooth?

There are some great suggestions in the "Tour Indiana" and "Sweets and Treats" sections in the back of the guide.

KANPAI

4593 Washington Avenue
Evansville, IN 47714
(812) 471-7076
www.mykanpai.com
Open daily for lunch and dinner.

The restaurant is small and unassuming in appearance, but on a Saturday morning at 11:00 am, 13 people were already in line. They weren't all from the immediate area either. Colorado-born Chef Munoz offers an imaginative sushi menu with selections as different as Dynamite and Yum Yum Rolls. There is an appealing Bento Box lunch menu and entrées that include stir frys, seared or blackened tuna and Chop Chae, which is sweet potato noodles with your choice of beef, chicken or shrimp. Save room for a banana wonton for dessert.

KELLY JAE'S CAFÉ

133 South Main Street
Goshen, IN 46526
(574) 537-1027
www.kellyjaescafe.com
Open Tuesday-Friday for lunch & dinner; Saturday for dinner.
Closed Sunday & Monday.

Kelly Jae creates tapas with an Asian flare. Sharing or not sharing the uniquely delicious small plates is up to you, but the menu states, "We don't want to see you pouting when you want a bite of everyone else's." In keeping with the commitment to use primarily locally-grown ingredients, each day has special offerings like a watermelon, feta cheese, and black olive combination. The menu includes starters, spreads, soups, side dishes, and cold and hot tapas. It is hard to call some of the entrées "small plates," like the Pad Thai and grilled blackened hanger steak with blue cheese fondue. The sharing of food, drinks and conversation can take place in either the bar or the dining room.

KEY WEST SHRIMP HOUSE

117 Ferry Street
Madison, IN 47250
(812) 265-2831
www.keywestshrimphouse.com
Open Tuesday-Sunday for lunch & dinner. Closed Monday.

Dine in an old button factory while overlooking the Ohio River. This small restaurant has been serving customers here for over 40 years. Shrimp is the specialty: coconut, orange grilled or fried. Frog legs, catfish, steak and chicken are also on the menu. An unlimited salad bar is offered at dinner. If you are in the area, the Shrimp House is a good place to eat and imagine what life was like in a town along the river.

KINSEY'S ITALIAN CAFÉ
6383 West Broadway
McCordsville, IN 46055
(317) 336-1300
www.kinseysitaliancafe.com
Open Monday-Saturday for lunch & dinner. Closed Sunday.

Kinsey's is a popular neighborhood spot for Italian food and there is always a full house. The pizza dough is special and it makes delicious knots that accompany the signature dishes. Other than pizza, highlights on the menu include the Panzerotti Calzone, the Kinsey's Meat Trio (lasagna, spaghetti & meatballs, and beef ravioli), and Kinsey's Feast that combines Italian sausage, chicken and shrimp, served over fettuccini. A customer applauded the friendly small town atmosphere on the outskirts of Indianapolis.

KITCHEN TABLE
15315 Old Lima Road
Huntertown, IN 46748
(260) 637-5190
www.kitchentablehuntertown.com
Open Monday-Friday for breakfast, lunch & dinner;
Saturday and Sunday for breakfast & lunch.

If you are looking for a small town auto repair shop and a place to eat while you wait for your car, go to the Kitchen Table in Huntertown. Myers Service Station was established in 1952 and the adjoining "small hometown restaurant" is a fun place to revisit the past, even if you aren't having your car repaired. The original counters and stools are still in use. The food is all homemade with daily specials like beef and noodles over mashed potatoes. This warm and inviting restaurant reflects a family owned establishment where original customers still make weekly visits.

KLEMM'S CANDLELIGHT CAFÉ
1207 East State Boulevard
Fort Wayne, IN 46805
(260) 471-6828
Open daily for breakfast & lunch.

You might be asking, "Why candlelight?" when only breakfast and lunch are served. The answer is simple...that was the original name of the restaurant and candlelights are still present in the back room. It is a good place to start the day and breakfast is served all day. With the exception of "garbage & toast" and "half & half," the usual breakfast items are offered. Homemade daily lunch specials include pan-fried chicken, but you might prefer one of the sandwiches, wraps, baskets, or salads. Customers report that Klemm's is a comfortable place to gather.

KLEPTZ'S RESTAURANT
9711 East U.S. Highway 40
Seelyville, IN 47878
(812) 877-2314
www.kleptzrestaurant.com
Open daily for lunch & dinner.

Built in 1902 to house a dry goods and grocery store, Frank Kleptz and his wife, Anna, converted the space into a bar/restaurant in 1920. Today, as you drive across US 40, equidistant from Brazil and Terre Haute, you can stop at Kleptz's and enjoy a varied menu that even includes bluegill and quail. We suggest a table in the bar area.

KONA JACK'S FISH MARKET & SUSHI BAR
9419 North Meridian Street
Indianapolis, IN 46260
(317) 843-1609 Ext. 6
www.jacksarebetter.net
Open Monday-Friday for lunch & dinner; Saturday for dinner. Closed Sunday.

Kona Jack's is not a "dining secret" to Indianapolis residents, but for visitors passing through via Interstate 465, a stop here is easily negotiated and is well worth it. You enter a tiki-type environment with colorful fish swimming in tanks around you. The fish market, in full view, entices diners to try the fresh fish specials, but the menu offers other choices, both land and sea. For those wanting to watch the process, seating in the sushi bar is available. Many people shop at the market and take seafood home. Upon request, suggestions for different preparations are enthusiastically offered by the staff.

KOPPER KETTLE INN
135 East Main Street
Morristown, IN 46161
(765) 763-6767
www.kopperkettle.com
Open Tuesday-Sunday for lunch & dinner. Closed Monday.

In business since 1923, the Kopper Kettle has a delightfully restful atmosphere where you can savor their famous Hoosier fried chicken, broiled prime steaks and delicious seafood, all served family-style. The large house is a veritable art museum, displaying a fascinating collection of art objects from many parts of the world. From the beautiful antique furnishings and artifacts to the balconies, fountains and strolling gardens, the Kopper Kettle has a distinctive charm unmatched in the area.

KOUNTRY KITCHEN SOUL FOOD PLACE
1831 North College Avenue
Indianapolis, IN 46221
(317) 926-4476
www.kountrykitchenindy.com
Open daily for breakfast, lunch and dinner.

The message printed on the wall is so true: "Kountry Kitchen focuses on placing customers in the center of everything we do by providing quality food and service in a family friendly atmosphere." People of all ages gather here to enjoy the very best southern cooking. Many items are made from scratch and, as the waitress explained with a hearty laugh, "We are not a fast food restaurant!" For breakfast, in addition to fluffy pancakes and French toast, there is cube steak with gravy and fried whiting filets. Lunch and dinner entrées include fried chicken, pork chops and homemade meat loaf. The sides add to the food that speaks to the soul: greens, okra, fried green tomatoes, grits, and your choice of fried or baked biscuits. Dessert specialties are banana pudding and "lip smacking cobbler." It's no wonder the walls are filled with pictures of celebrity visitors, including Barack Obama.

KUNKEL'S DRIVE-IN
2402 North Park Road
Connersville, IN 47331
(765) 825-9211
www.kunkelsdrivein.com
Open daily for lunch & dinner.

A bit of nostalgia awaits you at Kunkel's, an old-fashioned drive-in restaurant where you pull up to the speaker/tray station, push the button, place your order and await delivery. Choose a salad, soup, or a burger, tenderloin, fish tail, or pizza steak sandwich. The classics are also available: flavored soft drinks, milkshakes, malts, sodas and root beer floats. Kunkel's also offers homemade pies. The car hop delivers your food with a friendly smile and proudly explains that the drive-in has been there since 1954.

L.A. CAFÉ
4 South Main Street
Whitestown, IN 46075
(317) 769-7503
www.newlacafe.com

Open Monday-Saturday for lunch & dinner. Closed Sunday.

The motto is "let the good times roll," so when rolling into this small town, stop at the place where motorcycles are parked alongside a stretch limo. People from all walks of life are drawn to this eclectic destination restaurant. The inside is decorated in orange, black and chrome with motorcycle memorabilia everywhere. The family-friendly atmosphere is accentuated by white tablecloths covered with paper that children can color on while waiting for their meal. The menu begins with homemade soups, salads, and a fiery shrimp cocktail made with fresh horseradish. Entrées include hand-cut steaks, ribs, fresh fish, and daily seafood and pasta specials. The lunch menu features burgers, sandwiches, a "killer burrito" and various salads. Beverages include a complete line of beer, wine and spirits.

LA PARADA
1642 East New York
Indianapolis, IN 46201
(317) 917-0095
Open daily for lunch & dinner.

When you enter La Parada, you feel like you have stepped into Mexico, reflected by the pictures on the furniture and wall murals. The colorful red, blue, yellow and green decor attracts the eye and makes you smile. The staff is warm, friendly, and most helpful at ordering time. Assistance is necessary as the menu is extensive, from a drink called Horchata to a dessert called Elote. Tamales, tacos, and tortillas filled with different meats and seafood are the main courses. Several <u>Dining Secrets</u> readers suggest that La Parada has the most authentic Mexican food in Indianapolis.

LA SCALA RESTAURANT
312 Main Street
Lafayette, IN 47901
(765) 420-8171
www.lascalaitalianrestaurant.com
Open Monday-Friday for lunch & dinner; Saturday for dinner.
Closed Sunday.

You are invited to "eat fresh, eat well, eat local...eat La Scala!" A family effort converted an old "hole-in-the-wall" structure on the square in Lafayette into this popular restaurant with a bar and outdoor patio. Their "Farm to Fork" initiative grew out of another family commitment to provide customers with locally grown, chemically-free foods. There is a warm weather and cold weather menu. Whether you choose pasta your way or from the chef's specialty pastas, you can be sure your entrée is made fresh when you place your order. Soups, salads, sandwiches and pizzas are available.

LAKEHOUSE GRILLE
620 East Lake Shore Drive
Culver, IN 46511
(574) 842-2234
www.thelakehouseculver.com
Open Tuesday-Sunday for lunch & dinner. Closed Monday.

The Lakehouse has quite a collection of marine memorabilia: boats hang from the ceiling and surf boards, sailfish and paddles adorn the walls. Signs on display make you smile: "Maxinkuckee Mist—The Ale You Sailed On," "MAX WAX—surf board dressing AND hair pomade!" Booths in the bar have their own TVs and there are private booths in the dining room. Huge windows overlook Lake Maxinkuckee. The menu is comprehensive and you are sure to find a favorite. The hot artichoke dip, jumbo coconut shrimp, wild mushroom ravioli, steak or one of the nightly specials are all worth the trip. Sushi is available Thursday through Sunday.

LASALLE GRILL

115 West Colfax Avenue
South Bend, IN 46601
(574) 288-1155; (800) 382-9323
www.lasallegrill.com
Open Monday-Saturday for dinner. Closed Sunday.

LaSalle Grill has a well-deserved reputation for providing guests with a memorable dining experience in a lively, upscale atmosphere. The cuisine is modern American, a blend of many classic and ethnic ingredients using only the highest quality, freshest foods available. Items change daily to reflect the seasons and are designed to stimulate and intrigue the palate; the presentation is unique and creative. In addition to a superb selection of appetizers, desserts and an award-winning wine list, there is an outstanding choice of entrées: Maple Leaf Farms duck, hardwood grilled rack of lamb, and wood-fired prime steaks. You can also enjoy a more casual setting and dinner menu in the LaSalle Kitchen & Tavern, located on the third floor of the building and open Tuesday through Saturday evenings.

LATE HARVEST KITCHEN

8605 River Crossing Blvd.
Indianapolis, IN 46250
(317) 663-8063
www.lateharvestkitchen.com
Open for dinner Monday-Saturday. Closed Sunday

Escape the hubbub of Keystone at the Crossing in a contemporary restaurant on a corner of the Shops at River Crossing. On a nice evening, having a drink and appetizer outside on comfortable couches, surrounded by attractive greenery, is inviting. The dinner menu offers a delightful array of tastes. There are appetizer choices from crispy fried deviled eggs to goat cheese stuffed mushrooms. Daily entrees include a whole roasted fish or Alaskan halibut. Meats served are locally sourced and recipes have many combinations of flavors. The menu changes seasonally.

LAUGHING PLANET CAFÉ

322 East Kirkwood Avenue (at Grant Street)
Bloomington, IN 47408
(812) 323-2233
www.thelaughingplanetcafe.com
Open daily for lunch & dinner.

The spicy aroma draws you into this restaurant that majors in "whole foods in a hurry." After you place your order at the counter, you can enjoy a hearty laugh as you peruse the walls: hanging bikes with the sign "Get a life get a bike," bold and colorful paintings, dinosaur toys, a shrine with customer messages asking for divine assistance, a framed original Swanson TV dinner tray and much more. Nutritious burritos are the top sellers with a "How to Eat a Burrito" pictorial guide on each table. Burritos are stuffed with your choice of numerous ingredients. Incredible homemade soups are delicious. There are also salads and veggie burgers. You bus your own table and are encouraged not to be wasteful.

LEGEND CLASSIC IRVINGTON CAFÉ

5614 East Washington Street
Indianapolis, IN 46219
(317) 536-2028
www.thelegendcafe.com
Open Tuesday-Saturday for lunch & dinner; Sunday for brunch.
Closed Monday.

Why the "legend?" The Irvington neighborhood gets its name from Washington Irving, author of the "Legend of Sleepy Hollow," and this café is located in the heart of Irvington. There are daily specials, but the salads, soups and sandwiches, even a create your own sandwich, are always available for lunch. Hot entrées include Mom's Meatloaf and a B.B.B. (black bean burger). For dinner, beef tenderloin, dad's crunchy chicken, and pan fried walleye are among the tasty entrées. Made from scratch cookies are a good dessert choice. The Legend is a very comfortable neighborhood restaurant.

LEMON BAR

95 East Pine Street
Zionsville, IN 46077
(317) 418-7274
www.thelemonbaronline.com
Open Tuesday-Saturday for lunch & dinner; Sunday for brunch. Closed Monday.

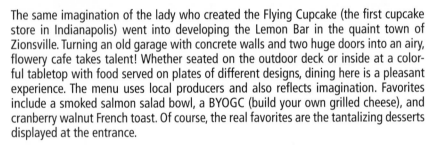

The same imagination of the lady who created the Flying Cupcake (the first cupcake store in Indianapolis) went into developing the Lemon Bar in the quaint town of Zionsville. Turning an old garage with concrete walls and two huge doors into an airy, flowery cafe takes talent! Whether seated on the outdoor deck or inside at a colorful tabletop with food served on plates of different designs, dining here is a pleasant experience. The menu uses local producers and also reflects imagination. Favorites include a smoked salmon salad bowl, a BYOGC (build your own grilled cheese), and cranberry walnut French toast. Of course, the real favorites are the tantalizing desserts displayed at the entrance.

LEMON DROP

1701 Mounds Road
Anderson, IN 46016
(765) 644-9055
Open Monday-Saturday for lunch & dinner. Closed Sunday.

The yellow exterior, basket of lemon drops and a cooler of lemonade would suggest reasons for the restaurant's name, but the fact is that the original owner was named Lemon. Not much has changed since the restaurant opened in 1954 and the staff and the clientele are proud of that history. The space is small with a few tables, a counter, a jukebox and an old red Coke machine. The parking lot that backs up to the train tracks is always full. Onion burgers (two hamburger patties with onions in between) and cheeseburgers on toast are the most popular sandwiches. Onion rings, french fries and milkshakes complete the meal. Be sure to take a lemon drop as you leave.

LIGHTHOUSE

7501 Constitution Avenue
Cedar Lake, IN 46303
(219) 374-9283
www.cedarlakelighthouse.com
Open Tuesday-Sunday for dinner.
Closed Monday. Call for seasonal hours.

The lighthouse beacon draws locals from the lake, along with visitors who appreciate the dining room's lakefront views while enjoying a meal. Others stop in to visit the old Century boat bar or view the history of Cedar Lake carefully recorded in photos on the walls. Of course, the food is also a reason to visit. The steaks, pork chops, lamb chops, lake perch and macadamia nut crusted walleye are good, but there are significant other options and some daily specials. Whatever your reason for seeking out the Lighthouse, you will not be disappointed.

LITTLE SHEBA'S

175 Fort Wayne Avenue
Richmond, IN 47374
(765) 962-2999
www.littleshebas.com
Open Monday-Saturday for lunch & dinner. Closed Sunday.

Located in Richmond's historic district, Little Sheba's used to be a butcher shop near the old train station. As a matter of fact, the old wooden meat locker door is still there. Choose from a variety of toppings and fillings in wraps, on pitas, breads or buns, along with sides of french fries and tasty homemade pasta or potato salad. On a nice day, you might enjoy a walk along the street to see some of the historic spots in the area.

LOCALLY GROWN GARDENS

1050 East 54th Street
Indianapolis, IN 46220
(317) 255-8555
www.locallygrowngardens.com
Open Tuesday-Sunday for lunch & dinner. Closed Monday.

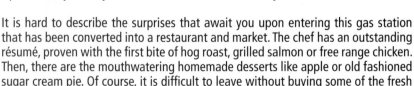

It is hard to describe the surprises that await you upon entering this gas station that has been converted into a restaurant and market. The chef has an outstanding résumé, proven with the first bite of hog roast, grilled salmon or free range chicken. Then, there are the mouthwatering homemade desserts like apple or old fashioned sugar cream pie. Of course, it is difficult to leave without buying some of the fresh produce or other specialty items displayed throughout the space.

LOFT AT TRADERS POINT CREAMERY

9101 Moore Road
Zionsville, IN 46077
(317) 733-1700
www.traderspointcreamery.com
Open Tuesday-Saturday for lunch & dinner; Sunday for brunch. Closed Monday.

It is hard to believe that this 100% grass-fed dairy in its idyllic surroundings is so easily accessible from Interstate 465. Plan to visit the dairy and Green Market at mealtime and experience the pleasure of eating a healthy meal in the country and of sampling the latest Traders Point Creamery products. The menu highlights each season's "fresh, simple and organic" products. There are cheese appetizers, a signature gouda vegetable soup, a strawberry fields salad and lunch sandwiches. The dinner entrées might include 100% grass-fed steak, fresh fish, or farm house mac 'n cheese. Whole milk ice creams of seasonal flavors are available for dessert. All of this can be enjoyed in a barn-like structure with fresh flowers on your table. The Loft is an authentic farm-to-table restaurant.

LOG INN

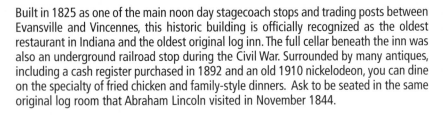

12491 South 200 East
Off I-64 on Warrenton Road
Haubstadt, IN 47639
(812) 867-3216
www.theloginn.net
Open Tuesday-Saturday for dinner. Closed Sunday & Monday.
CASH AND CHECKS ONLY.

Built in 1825 as one of the main noon day stagecoach stops and trading posts between Evansville and Vincennes, this historic building is officially recognized as the oldest restaurant in Indiana and the oldest original log inn. The full cellar beneath the inn was also an underground railroad stop during the Civil War. Surrounded by many antiques, including a cash register purchased in 1892 and an old 1910 nickelodeon, you can dine on the specialty of fried chicken and family-style dinners. Ask to be seated in the same original log room that Abraham Lincoln visited in November 1844.

LOS COTORROS

3901 West State Road 47
Sheridan, IN 46069
(317) 758-6728
Open daily for lunch & dinner.

Tucked away in the small town of Sheridan is a restaurant that offers big time taste in authentic Mexican fare. The usual burritos, fajitas, chimichangas and quesadillas are on the menu, but ingredients have been added that make these choices unique. Special, out-of-the-ordinary items like scallops chalupa, steak toluqueno, chicken (pollo) fundido and chile verde may tempt you. All meals are served by a very gracious staff who are eager to have you enjoy their food. The margaritas are good, too.

LUCKY LOU SEAFOOD AND DIM SUM

3623 Commercial Drive
Indianapolis, IN 46222
(317) 293-8888
Open Monday, Tuesday & Thursday-Sunday for lunch & dinner. Closed Wednesday.

Lucky Lou's has the reputation for serving authentic Chinese food. The menu is quite extensive but well organized and easily navigated. Choose the desired meat or vegetable and then select what you want to put with it. There are Szechuan dishes, stir frys and chef specialties. The unique offering at Lucky Lou's is dim sum which is served everyday, but on Saturday and Sunday you can order off a cart that circulates the restaurant. Dim sum is small plates and good to share with others. The dim sum menu has good pictures and descriptions, which helps when choosing what to order. Weekend dim sum has some items not included during the week, like the custard puffs and pork rolls.

LUCREZIA

428 South Calumet Road
Chesterton, IN 46304
(219) 926-5829
www.lucreziacafé.com
Open daily for lunch & dinner.

Was the famous Lucrezia Borgia a patron of the arts or a depraved woman? Is her reputation for wantonness and crime legend more than fact? What we do know is that she would appreciate and enjoy the food at this restaurant bearing her name. A picture of Lucrezia, painted by a local artist, greets you as you enter and overlooks the bar where martinis are the specialty. The dining rooms are small and intimate, accented with marble table tops and wood floors. Blackboards on the wall announce the daily specials: fish, pasta, chicken, salads, and vegetables. Pastas are available in many combinations, and the fish, lamb, salmon and veal entrées are truly special. For dessert, you may want to try the seasonal stuffed strawberries or the homemade tiramisu.

LULU'S COFFEE + BAKEHOUSE

2292 West 86th Street
Indianapolis, IN 46260
(317) 879-1995
www.luluscoffeeandbakehouse.com
Open daily for breakfast & lunch.

What a pleasant place to start the day or meet a friend for lunch. The hospitable staff takes great pride in the product, which is everything fresh baked daily: breads, muffins, scones, cookies, brownies, pies, etc. Breakfast egg dishes, soups and salads complement the homemade baked goods. Being close to the hospital, there is a St. Vincent's Hummus Plate. A nice assortment of coffee and non-coffee beverages is available.

MADELEINE'S
423 SE Second Street
Evansville, IN 47713
(812) 491-8611
www.madeleinesfusion.com
Open Tuesday-Saturday for dinner. Closed Sunday & Monday.

Fusion, as it applies to food, means a blending or melding together of flavors and Madeleine's prides itself on being Evansville's fusion restaurant. The chef presents the freshest fish, meat and vegetables and prepares them with a creative flair. Dinners are three course meals: first, an appetizer such as chicken satay; second, soup or salad; third, an entrée like the pan-roasted sea bass with Veracruz rock shrimp and cauliflower risotto. The unique and flavorful choices on the menu change weekly.

MADISON'S
104 West State Street
Pendleton, IN 46064
(765) 221-9390
www.madisonsind.com
Open Tuesday-Saturday for dinner. Sunday for brunch. Closed Monday.

A Virginia Woolf quote on Madison's wall sets the mood for dining: "One cannot think well, love well, sleep well if one has not dined well." Though the restaurant describes itself as "unpretentious," the chef-owner's menu includes creative mixtures of flavors and ingredients. The owners take pride in using locally grown produce and presenting delectable homemade desserts. Wine tasting events and craft cocktails are also advertised.

MAMA CAROLLA'S
1031 East 54th Street
Indianapolis, IN 46220
(317) 259-9412
www.mamacarollas.com
Open Tuesday-Saturday for dinner. Closed Sunday & Monday.

With a desire to authenticate the look of the Italian "mom and pop" restaurants of Omaha, Nebraska, the owners of Mama Carolla's found what they were looking for in this 1920s California stucco, Mediterranean-style home. Wrought iron and white brick create the feeling of dining in a café, terrace restaurant, or a lovely home in Spain or Italy. Entrées offer a choice of steak, veal, chicken, salmon, tuna or uniquely tasty pasta dishes. Specialties include pasta carbonara, chicken rigatoni, rosemary chicken lasagna and Uncle Dino's or Cousin Mary's steak. For dessert lovers, there's tiramisu, cannoli, or a dish of spumoni.

MAMA'S KOREAN RESTAURANT

8867 Pendleton Pike
Indianapolis, IN 46226
(317) 897-0808
www.indymamarestaurant.com
Open daily for lunch & dinner. Closed between lunch & dinner.

Mama's Korean Restaurant

Mama's presents a workable, comfortable menu written in Korean, followed by simple, succinct English explanations. Additional information suggests the customer is his/her own chef choosing the entrée. Then, there is good advice in selecting the amazing and numerous side dishes called Banchan that complete the meal. Some tables have built-in BBQ grills, enabling diners to cook their own meats and then dip and mix with the selected sides. Helpers provide guidance for those who are unfamiliar with the spiciness of Korean food. House prepared plated dishes that do not require work on your part are also available. A visit to Mama's feels like a trip to another country and offers a positive exposure to the food.

MARKET STREET GRILL

90 West Market
Wabash, IN 46992
(260) 563-7779
www.msgrill.com
Open Tuesday-Friday for lunch & dinner; Saturday for dinner.
Closed Sunday & Monday.

The interior of this restaurant reflects the owner's interest in trains and antiques. Lots of memorabilia covers the brick walls and creates a backdrop for the electric train that travels throughout the restaurant. You can enjoy a drink or a bottle of beer delivered in an ice bucket while waiting in one of the old barber chairs. Begin your meal with bacon, lettuce and tomato soup, followed by one of the house specialties: "drunk'in chicken," prime rib or barbecued ribs. In addition to steaks and seafood, the menu offers a nice selection of low fat entrées, sandwiches, and their award-winning chili. You must be at least 18 and accompanied by a 21-year-old to enter.

MATTEO'S RISTORANTE ITALIANO

40 North 9th Street
Noblesville, IN 46060
(317) 774-9771
www.matteosindy.com
Open Monday-Friday for lunch & dinner; Saturday & Sunday for dinner.

The owners, a couple who met at Dining Secrets' Capri restaurant, wanted to bring the tastes of Salerno, Italy to a town close to the city but still be able to draw from the country. They chose the square in Noblesville and created an inviting atmosphere with high ceilings, chandeliers, dark wood and warm colors. Crusty bread with a nicely seasoned olive oil is presented by an enthusiastic staff as you peruse the chef/owner's creative menu. Antipasti insalate, meat, fish, chicken and pasta main courses, along with an assortment of sides, are offered, plus a variety of specials and a "speed lunch" option. Family-style meals for parties or groups are also available.

MAXINE'S CHICKEN & WAFFLES

132 North East Street
Indianapolis, IN 46204
(317) 423-3300
www.maxineschicken.com
Open Tuesday-Sunday for breakfast, lunch & dinner. Closed Monday.

Maxine's was built by a close-knit family to honor their mother Maxine, a cook at St. Francis Hospital for 30 years. The restaurant's motto, "Taste of love in every bite," captured her desire to make tasty dishes mixing vegetables from the garden and wild game. Omelets and egg dishes are on the breakfast menu, but the waffle with fried chicken wings is hard to beat. Of course, the waffle can also be topped with peach butter and syrup. Along with fish, chicken that is fried, grilled, in a salad or in sausage can be ordered. Fried green tomatoes, grits, rice with gravy, and collard greens are among the many side dishes and are included with the fish and chicken dinner entrées.

MAYBERRY CAFÉ

78 West Main Street
Danville, IN 46122
(317) 745-4067
Open daily for breakfast, lunch & dinner.

If you're a fan of the Andy Griffith Show, head to the town square in Danville and look for the squad car parked out front. You will appreciate the many pictures and other memorabilia from the television classic that decorate the interior of this small town restaurant. The café-type decor includes lace tablecloths, brass chandeliers and an Aunt Bee's parlor atmosphere. A little of the big city charm is noticeable in the 40-50 item menu offering ribeye, orange roughy, prime rib, fried chicken and catfish. Make sure you save room for a piece of Aunt Bee's apple pie.

McCLURE'S ORCHARD/WINERY

5054 North U.S. Hwy. 31
Peru, IN 46970
(765) 985-9000
www.mccluresorchard.com
Open Tuesday-Sunday for lunch & early dinner. Closed Monday.

This is an apple orchard by name but so much more. Visit the Apple Dumplin' Inn where the chicken salad is served with applesauce and the pork loin is applewood smoked. Of course, biscuits and apple butter accompany the meal. The entrées are good, but you must save room for the delicious apple dumpling served with apple crisp ice cream. Before or after your meal, you can stroll around the grounds and enjoy the activities: wine tasting and shopping for apples, apple products, holiday decorations and gifts. Children will enjoy visiting the animal barn, riding ponies and climbing at the playground. McClure's is a destination with something for everyone to enjoy.

MCGRAW'S STEAK, CHOP & FISH HOUSE
2707 South River Road
West Lafayette, IN 47906
(765) 743-3932
www.mcgrawssteakhouse.com
Open Tuesday-Saturday for dinner. Closed Sunday & Monday.

As you wind down South River Road, a lighted fishing boat marks the place to turn into this establishment. It is close to Fort Ouiatenon. The catfish on the menu is the only evidence of what used to be called Stiney's Restaurant. Today, there is an inviting atmosphere with a brightly polished wood floor, comfortable bar and a tantalizing menu. Appetizers vary from fried shoestring onions to poached shrimp martinis. Salad choices include the black and blue steak and fall harvest salad. Tempting entrées feature great steaks, sauteed walleye, chicken McGraw, and the prime rib special is reported to be unique.

MERIDIAN
5694 North Meridian
Indianapolis, IN 46208
(317) 466-1111
www.meridianonmeridian.com
Open Monday-Saturday for lunch & dinner; Sunday for dinner.

The Meridian is named for its location on Indianapolis' most famous and easily accessible thoroughfare, Meridian Street. This big old house, just a short walk from Broad Ripple and across from the canal, has been serving food and drink to Hoosiers and travelers for almost a century. Whether you eat on the patio, in the dining room by the fireplace, or at the bar, the Meridian is a comfortable place to enjoy lunch or dinner. In addition to sandwiches and salads, items such as fish tacos and quiche Lorraine are wonderful lunch options. The dinner menu has a nice choice of fish, chicken, lamb, pork and beef entrées, each served with outstanding accompaniments.

MILKTOOTH
534 Virginia Avenue
Indianapolis, IN 46203
(317) 986-5131
www.milktoothindy.com
Open Wednesday-Monday for breakfast & lunch. Closed Tuesday.

When you pull into the parking lot, you get the feeling this could have been an auto repair shop, but now there is a garden and outdoor furniture in front of the garage doors. As you walk inside, you see stools at the counter, church lights, thick wooden tables, coffee and cracker cans with silverware on each table, and it all exudes a comfortable atmosphere. The menu features an interesting, diverse selection of breakfast and lunch items, and quite a variety of specialty coffees, teas and cocktails.

M. MOGGER'S BREWERY EATERY & PUB

908 Poplar Street
Terre Haute, IN 47802
(812) 234-9202
www.moggers-restaurant.com
Open daily for lunch & dinner.

Take a trip back to the past as you enter this old brewery named after Matthias Mogger, a German immigrant. The E. Bleemel Building, built in 1837, housed Mogger's Brewery from 1848 to 1868 and is a significant part of early beer brewing history in the Wabash Valley. The floors, woodwork and dumbwaiter that carried barrels from the basement to the store level, along with other brewing paraphernalia, create a unique dining atmosphere. Today, Mogger's has over 170 beers to choose from and offers an MBA (Masters of Beer Appreciation). There are many choices of burgers, sandwiches, steak, seafood, pork and pasta entrées, plus soups and salad dressings that are homemade. The Italian beef sandwich and the drunken cod are reported to be excellent.

MUG N BUN

5211 West 10th Street
Speedway, IN 46224
(317) 244-5669
www.mug-n-bun.com
Open daily for lunch & dinner.

Take a step back and enjoy reliving the past at this well-known, west side drive-in that has been a fixture in Speedway for almost 50 years. Turn on your headlights or press a button on the picnic table and a waitress will appear to take your order. The Mug N Bun is an independent root beer maker with a brew that is full-bodied, tangy and served in a frosted mug. You can enjoy a breaded tenderloin, BBQ sandwich, hamburger, hand-dipped onion rings that are cut fresh daily, root beer float, or other drive-in specialties, but several items stand out as being unique: mini corndogs, sweet potato fries with sugar and cinnamon, and delicious fried apple crescents.

MURPHY'S at FLYNN'S

5198 North Allisonville Road
Indianapolis, IN 46205
(317) 545-3707
www.murphyssteakhouse.com
Open Monday-Friday for lunch & dinner; Saturday for dinner. Closed Sunday.

Tradition, family, loyalty and good food made a name for both Murphy's and Flynn's. The two restaurants merged in 2014, combining the best of both establishments. Along with pub fare, there is seafood, steaks and chops. Note the specials on the blackboard as you enter. Entrées include choices of sides and the homemade salad dressings are highly recommended. It is a friendly, comfortable place to dine and there is a camaraderie among the staff that reflects the years of commitment to serving patrons in these neighborhood restaurants.

NAPOLI VILLA

758 Main Street
Beech Grove, IN 46107
(317) 783-4122
www.napoliindy.com
Open Monday-Friday for lunch & dinner; Saturday for dinner. Closed Sunday.

Napoli Villa first opened its doors in 1962 to Italian immigrants. Today, the same family operates the restaurant, continuing the traditions that made this trattoria so popular. Upon entering the restaurant, the old world aromas of the fresh tomato sauce send you back to Italy. There is a nice variety of pastas, pizzas and sandwiches. For the more adventurous, a wide range of gourmet dishes are offered, such as the Gambarella (shrimp) alla Romana and Pollo alla Cacciatore. Don't forget to save room for dolce—a mouthwatering selection of traditional and contemporary desserts.

NASHVILLE HOUSE

15 South VanBuren Street
Nashville, IN 47448
(812) 988-4554
Open Wednesday-Monday for lunch & dinner.
Closed Tuesdays.

An Indiana restaurant guide would not be complete without mentioning the Nashville House, famous for its fried biscuits with homemade apple butter. Originally the site of a hotel built in 1859, that structure burned down and was rebuilt in 1947, housing a restaurant and country store. Native Brown County woodwork, red and white checked tablecloths, and a wonderful collection of antiques decorate the interior. Lunch features sandwiches served on homemade bread and daily specials. Country fried chicken, ham, and turkey dinners are available all day. Special homemade desserts include the famous pecan nut pie, cobblers and cream pies.

NEW ALBANIAN BREWING COMPANY, PIZZERIA & PUBLIC HOUSE

3312 Plaza Drive
New Albany, IN 47150
(812) 944-2577
www.newalbanian.com
Open Monday-Saturday for lunch & dinner. Closed Sunday.

This establishment is a brewery, pizzeria and bar all rolled into one. Beers are brewed in the garage and advertised on big blackboards, boasting that, "There is no such thing as light beer here!" The beers are special but the pizza is truly unique. Where have you ever been offered from 5 to 10 toppings for one price? Before selecting from the list of 20-plus ingredients, you have to decide whether you want your pie hand-tossed, roundhouse (deep dish), upside down (sauce on the bottom), or "refrigerator," which is twice the amount of toppings. While you'e here, check out the beer trivia on the walls.

NEXT DOOR AMERICAN EATERY

4573 North College Avenue
Indianapolis, IN 46205
(317) 643-3480
www.nextdooreatery.com
Open daily for lunch & dinner.

Located on the corner of 46th and College, some locals might remember it being a Kroger or a Double 8. A sign over the kitchen promises "Scratch Cooking," and a daily sandwich board informs diners as to what is on the menu. In addition to snacks to share, there are sandwiches, burgers, salads, bowls and soups. A salmon bowl includes kale, beets, quinoa and lemon. Items are identified as gluten free, dairy free, vegan, and vegetarian. There are zero proof cocktails in addition to the usual bar options.

NICK'S KITCHEN

506 North Jefferson
Huntington, IN 46750
(260) 356-6618
www.nickskitchen.net
Open Monday & Tuesday for breakfast & lunch;
Wednesday-Saturday for breakfast, lunch & dinner. Closed Sunday.

In the morning or at lunchtime, Nick's proclaims, "We don't do fast food. We just do great food fast!" Dan Quayle's hometown campaign visits made people aware of Nick's and the famous breaded tenderloin that "you need both hands to eat!" Historic photos of the town decorate the walls. A breakfast bowl with eggs, potatoes, bacon, and sausage gravy that you eat with a spoon is a popular choice. For lunch, there is the "original" breaded tenderloin, a Quayle burger with fries, a margherita pizza, plus hand-dipped shakes and fresh baked pies. You will enjoy people-watching as the local citizens gather around the community table, complete with atlases and dictionaries, to settle friendly disagreements about the facts.

NICOLE TAYLOR'S BACK ROOM EATERY

1134 East 54th Street, Studio C
Indianapolis, IN 46220
(317) 257-7374
www.nicoletaylorspasta.com
Open for lunch Tuesday-Saturday. Market is open until 6 pm weekdays.

"Dining Secrets" is announcing that the Back Room at Nicole Taylor's market is indeed a well-kept secret. Upon entering, the customer is faced with cases of fresh made pasta, sauces, salads and sweets. A blackboard at the counter suggests there is a menu for ordering soup, sandwiches and salads, but there are no visible tables until you go around the corner to the back room. The tables provide a view of the pasta-making process. Each place setting has a napkin carefully tied with a string, and a bowl of zesty popcorn is available for munching. The sandwiches with fresh, creatively combined ingredients are served on tasty bread. Choose any soup that Chef Hanslits has created and you will not be disappointed. For dessert, a cannoli with or without chocolate is recommended.

NINE MILE RESTAURANT

13398 U.S. Hwy 27 South
Fort Wayne, IN 46816
(260) 639-8112
www.ninemilerestaurant.com
Open Monday-Saturday for breakfast, lunch & dinner; Sunday for lunch & dinner.

A primitive tavern was established on this site in 1837, giving the Nine Mile Restaurant the right to advertise as the "oldest bar in Indiana." Today, there are very complete menus for all three meals. For breakfast, there are "Rise 'n Shine" sandwiches, home fries with gravy, and cinnamon and raisin toast. A comprehensive lunch and dinner menu features a variety of appetizers, soups, salads, specialty sandwiches and pizza, along with entrées of steak, baby back ribs, chicken and seafood. The restaurant prides itself in offering Waynedale Bakery pies for dessert. Full service catering is also available. Why is it called the Nine Mile Restaurant? Nine miles from what? Be sure to ask when you visit.

NISBET INN

6701 Nisbet Road (I-64, Exit 18)
Haubstadt, IN 47639
(812) 963-9305
Open Tuesday-Saturday for lunch & dinner. Closed Sunday & Monday.

Located at the site of an old railroad crossing about 10 miles north of Evansville, the Inn was built in 1912 as an oasis offering food, drink and lodging to the rail traveler. Even though a train hasn't passed through since 1971, the architecture has remained true to its original design, and it is still a popular place for food and drink. You will enjoy an atmosphere of warmth and hospitality where you can easily imagine yourself in an earlier and more relaxed time. Its reputation draws patrons from all over to sample some of the best barbecue around, along with a variety of sandwiches, homemade soups and pies. Claiming the "world's coldest beer," they have a nice selection of beer, wine and cocktails.

NO. 9 GRILL

27 West Main Street
Cambridge City, IN 47327
(765) 334-8315
www.no9grill.com
Open daily for lunch & dinner.

Traveling the national road through Indiana (U.S. 40) in many cases offers a living history of life in the Midwest: old homes, farms, cemeteries, stagecoach stops, and at least one store in every town selling antiques. No. 9 Grill is a comfortable place to stop and eat along the way. For many years the building housed the Masonic Lodge. The space has been nicely renovated with the town history preserved on walls filled with photographs. The menu carries a warning, "Not weight-loss compliant," and for the most part, it is not. There is a familiar assortment of appetizers, salads, sandwiches and steaks, with a few surprises like mac n' cheese bites.

NOAH GRANT'S GRILL HOUSE & OYSTER BAR
91 South Main Street
Zionsville, IN 46077
(317) 732-2233
www.noahgrants.com
Open Tuesday-Sunday for dinner. Closed Monday.

Dining Secrets has followed Noah Grant's for years. The current location on Zionsville's Main Street is clearly the best. The high ceilings, jellyfish streamer lights, coral pictured cushions and white and blue colors bring thoughts of seafood to mind. Oysters are available, even in non "r" months, and seafood is offered as starters or entrees. The chowders are delicious. For landlubbers, there is steak, meatloaf and chicken. Other venues within Noah Grant's are the "seafood bar" complete with black and white tiled floor, and the outdoor dining space in good weather.

NOOK
15 East Maryland Street
Indianapolis, IN 46204
(317) 759-3554
www.nookpaleo.com
Open Monday-Saturday for lunch & dinner. Closed Sunday.

The Nook's mission is to connect people to their food story. What does that mean? It is to combine fresh products with ethnic spices, such as American, Italian, Indian or Asian, to present choices that are compatible with customers' tastes, diets, allergies and other needs. That is a tall order, but accomplished in a casual fine dining environment with a menu that includes paleo friendly "angry shrimp tacos," vegan cobb salad, gluten friendly burgers and pizza, and keto-friendly bacon chips with guacamole. The Nook provides a healthy dining experience in a warm and welcoming atmosphere.

OAKLEYS BISTRO
1464 West 86th Street
Indianapolis, IN 46260
(317) 824-1231
www.oakleysbistro.com
Open Tuesday-Saturday for lunch & dinner. Closed Sunday & Monday.

Oakleys is a culinary pleasure enjoyed in comfortable surroundings. The food reflects the creative experience of chef-proprietor Steve Oakley, gained while working at famous restaurants in New York City and Chicago. The menu is designed to be "seasonal and innovative" so it changes regularly, but dishes are always prepared with the freshest products available. The presentation is like a picture, inviting you to taste and enjoy. Possible lunch items include lobster pot pie or wild boar sloppy joe. Along with a tempting selection of dinner appetizers, typical entrées might feature salmon, pork and duck. Indulge in a dessert after your meal.

OCTAVE GRILL

137 South Calumet Road
Chesterton, IN 46304
(219) 395-8494
Open daily for lunch & dinner.
Open mid-afternoon Monday-Friday.

Why the restaurant is called Octave is a story in itself. Octave Chanute (1832-1910), a French American civil engineer credited with designing Chicago's Union Stockyards, developed a fascination with the invention of the airplane during his retirement. He conducted aviation experiments with gliders off the Indiana dunes and published "Progress in Flying Machines" in 1894. Octave became an advisor to the Wright Brothers and pictures in the restaurant document the relationship of the first airplane to the Dunes gliders. The menu reflects a lot of imagination with entrées like the perch cake dinner. They are also known for their burgers where you take the basic and add unique toppings, such as fig jam and Capriole cheese. Creative alcoholic drinks are available.

OLD COLONIAL INN

216 North 3rd Street
Kentland, IN 47951
(219) 474-6774
www.oldcolonialinn.com
Open Thursday, Friday & Saturday for dinner. Closed Sunday-Wednesday.

If you are visiting Indiana's county courthouses or taking an alternate route to Chicago, a stop at the Old Colonial Inn is a highly touted dining opportunity. The restaurant is located in the renovated Hotel Kentland, which dates back to 1894. People from all over the state have suggested that the Inn is a definite "dining secret." The dinner menu includes prime rib, superb steaks, pork shank, chicken, walleye, lake perch, and much more. The service is excellent and the surroundings are warm and comfortable.

OLDE RICHMOND INN

138 South Fifth Street
Richmond, IN 47374
(765) 962-2247
www.olderichmondinn.com
Open daily for lunch & dinner.

This former 1892 residence exhibits the work of local "south-end Dutch" craftsmen and masons. The Victorian setting is accented with Italian decorative tiles, a stained glass wall from the 1800s, and stained glass fixtures designed by Richmond and Cincinnati craftsmen. A unique chandelier from the home of Micajah Henley, the inventor of roller skates, lights the north dining room, and three fireplaces add to the warm and inviting atmosphere. Special meals are prepared daily and served in a gracious and professional manner. To whet the appetite, sample the shrimp bianca appetizer, a house specialty. The American and continental-style menu offers a variety of prime cut steaks, seafood, chicken and pasta entrées for dinner; salads, sandwiches and chef's casserole of the day for lunch; and many daily blackboard specials. There is seasonal al fresco dining on the patio, and on-site banquet facilities are available for private parties.

ONE TEN CRAFT MEATERY

110 North Buffalo Street
Warsaw, IN 46580
(574) 267-7007
www.110craftmeatery.com
Open Wednesday-Friday for lunch & dinner; Saturday for dinner.
Closed Sunday, Monday and Tuesday.

As you enter the restaurant, located across from the county courthouse, there is a huge wall map of Indiana and the surrounding states. This informs diners that 110 is a farm-to-table restaurant where grass-fed and organic produce from these areas is served. The friendly staff welcomes you in tee shirts that say "Graze Local" and seat you at wooden tables topped with old glass milk bottles filled with water. The mood is set for the tasty menu, limited in item numbers but loaded with options based on what products are available. For appetizers there is a charcuterie block, hummus, or assorted bacons with biscuits and jam. There are meat and bread choices for hamburgers and sandwiches. Salads have numerous fresh ingredients, and dressings meet all tastes and desires. The entrées are perfectly prepared and accompanied by two side dishes. One person who dines out regularly and is considered a "food critic" claims that the 110 pork chop was the best he's ever had!

OPA!

7900 East US Highway 36
Avon, IN 46123
(317) 707-7513
www.opaavonin.com
Open daily for lunch & dinner.

If authentic Greek American cuisine is your desire, then Opa is the place. Though right off Highway 36, the high ceiling, sandy ocean walls, and open air seating create the feeling of being on a Greek island. An appetizer sample plate is a good start with pita, cucumbers, tomatoes, sauces, hummus, olives, etc. The menu includes traditional specialties with lamb, poultry and pork; however, there are also Opa burgers, Greek quesadillas and pasta dishes. For dessert, the traditional baklava is offered but the Olympic Flames, ice cream with the preserves of choice flamed with rum, is another great option.

OPERA HOUSE PUB

202 South Anderson Street
Elwood, IN 46036
(765) 557-2224
Open Monday-Saturday for lunch & dinner.
Closed Sunday.

The space has housed a drugstore and the Elwood Masonic Lodge, but the opera house history is what is celebrated. Vaudeville acts dating back to the late 1800s were presented on the upstairs stage of this restaurant. President McKinley, Wendell Willkie and Robert Kennedy (along with a history of a few ghosts) have visited this well-preserved site. The pub menu is presented in sections: Opening Acts (appetizers), Supporting Characters (burgers), Co-stars (pizzas and salads), Main Attractions (daily specials), and Curtain Calls (desserts). The upstairs Opera House still features stage performances and is available for special events.

OVERLOOK

1153 West State Road 62
(3 Miles South of I-64, Exit 92)
Leavenworth, IN 47137
(812) 739-4264
www.theoverlook.com
Open daily for lunch & dinner.

Overlooking a sweeping panorama of forested hills and the Ohio River as it arches around a horseshoe bend, you will enjoy magnificent views from every window in this appropriately named restaurant. The Overlook has earned a reputation over the years for good home cooking at very reasonable prices, offered in a warm and casual setting. Specialties include the popular creamed chicken served over homemade biscuits and a terrific beef manhattan. Steak, country fried chicken, ham, pork chops and seafood are additional selections. A nice variety of sandwiches is also available.

OWLERY

118 West 6th Street
Bloomington, IN 47404
(812) 333-7344
Open Monday-Saturday for lunch & dinner. Brunch on Sunday.

There is no shortage of restaurants on Bloomington's downtown square, each unique in its own way. The Owlery's specialty is vegetarian comfort food, craft beer, vegan baked goods, and the willingness to make any menu item vegan and some gluten-free. The daily offerings appear on the blackboard and the soup or stew of the day is highly recommended. Lunch sandwiches vary from tofu bacon, lettuce and tomato to red onion jam with cheddar cheese. Dinner might be a meal of three sides, pierogies, or even fried chicken. There is a multitude of owls watching over the small café.

OYSTER BAR

1830 South Calhoun
Fort Wayne, IN 46802
(260) 744-9490
www.fortwayneoysterbar.com
Open Monday-Friday for lunch & dinner; Saturday for dinner.
Closed Sunday.

A saloon that had been operating since 1888 was purchased in 1954 by Hughie Johnston, a local superstar athlete. He introduced oysters to the menu, but it wasn't until 1975 that the name became "The Oyster Bar." It feels like you have taken a step back in time as you view the sea memorabilia and Fort Wayne historical pictures decorating the interior. The bar, which surrounds an old cooler, is wonderfully inviting and customers can sit on the stools and eat their meals. A blackboard behind the bar lists the daily specials. Oysters can be prepared any way you want, and fresh fish is flat grilled, oven roasted, cedar planked, pan sauteed or naked, which is oven-broiled in lemon butter. For non-seafood eaters there are options such as pork tenderloin, barbecued ribs, lamb and pecan chicken.

PANGEA KITCHEN

111 South Green River Road
Evansville, IN 47715
(812) 401-2405
www.tastepangea.com
Open Tuesday-Saturday for lunch & dinner.
Closed Sunday & Monday

Pangea's Kitchen is a unique way to sample flavors from around the world and enjoy foods of different cultures all in one place. If Neapolitan (wood fired) or Detroit (deck oven) pizza is your choice, this is a good place to visit. Thai noodle dishes are also on the menu, along with Italian and Mexican inspired options. Complete your meal with a European-style dessert, such as French macarons, Italian cannolis and biscotti, or choose from the multiple flavors of gelato, served as dips, cones, pops or sandwiches.

PAPA'S

824 North Lakeshore Drive
Culver, IN 46511
(574) 842-3331
www.indianasbestpizza.com
Open Monday-Friday for dinner; Saturday & Sunday for lunch & dinner.

Papa Jim McCormack designed record album covers and promoted many of the hit groups that he came in contact with during the 1960s. In the early '70s, his Chicago family began to vacation in Culver, and in 1976, he opened this restaurant at Lake Maxinkuckee. Today, the walls are filled with music-related memorabilia, reminding us of PaPa's interests so many years ago. Build your own pasta or create your own pizza. There is a daily fresh catch and a featured cut of meat each week. Whether you are dining inside or out, you are surrounded by the lake atmosphere. Papa's is truly a "Culver institution."

PAPA ROUX

8950 East 10th Street
Indianapolis, IN 46219
(317) 603-9861
www.paparouxindy.com
Open Monday-Saturday for lunch & dinner. Closed Sunday.

Walk in and you are at the counter, ready to place your order for a Po-Boy, stew or the daily special. Po-Boys are "over a pound of goodness disguised as a sandwich." Ingredients include French bread filled with chicken, pork, roast beef, shrimp, sausage, or smoked ham, topped with their special recipe Vouxdoux Sauce and southern coleslaw. Stews include creoles, etouffee, chili, red beans and rice. Jambalaya and gumbo are also available. Sides are free with the meal and are ordered by raising the small flag on your table. The graffiti-filled brick walls, shared tables, unique chairs, and French word signs create a fun and friendly atmosphere.

PATACHOU

4901 North Pennsylvania
Indianapolis, IN 46205
(317) 925-2823
www.patachouinc.com
Open daily for lunch & dinner.

Patachou restaurants have been in Indianapolis since 1989. For good reason, they have received local, regional and national accolades for what has proven to be a well-designed food preparation and distribution plan. The Pennsylvania Street Patachou was the first, and it is clearly a neighborhood institution where people gather to conduct business, celebrate accomplishments, catch up with friends etc. while enjoying a quality healthy meal. Make-your-own breakfast omelettes are popular, as is oatmeal or broken yolks. For lunch, there are soups, salads and sandwiches that offer gluten-free bread as a choice. Ingredients come from local farms and producers within 100 miles. Patachou also maintains a Foundation where meals are provided to nourish and educate about healthy food choices.

PAULA'S ON MAIN

1732 West Main Street
Fort Wayne, IN 46808
(260) 424-2300

Open Monday-Friday for lunch & dinner; Saturday for dinner. Closed Sunday.

This old factory building is a great setting for an upscale casual dining experience. Fish is the highlight, as you will note from the on-site fresh seafood market, the decor and the menu. With the market and the motif, it feels like you are eating at a restaurant down at the docks. The daily features, listed on a separate sheet, are highly recommended. In addition to seafood appetizers and salads, the lunch entrées include walleye, salmon, jambalaya, trout and whitefish. Additional offerings for dinner include grouper, cioppino (bouillabaisse), lake perch piccata and lobster, along with chicken and steak selections.

PAYNE'S
4925 Kaybee Drive
Gas City, IN 46933
(765) 998-0668
www.paynescoffeeandcustard.com
Open daily for breakfast, lunch & dinner. (Call for breakfast times.)

Payne's is just one block east of Interstate 69, but there is no place like it for miles around. The owner is from Yorkshire, England, thus the Union Jack flag on the sign out front. Inside, a huge Pizza King arrow hangs over the small, comfortable seating area. For breakfast, there is French toast, oatmeal with everything, and a variety of coffee choices. Many lunch and dinner selections are prepared with a British flair, such as beef stew, Yorkshire pudding, and fish 'n chips. Bangers and mash, bruschetta, and fattoush are more options from other cultures. Wonderful custards complete this remarkable menu.

PEA-FECTIONS
321-323 Main Street
Vincennes, IN 47591
(812) 886-9177, (812) 886-5146
www.pea-fections.com
Open Monday-Saturday for lunch. Closed Sunday.

Pea is the owner's name, not the food focus. While in downtown Vincennes visiting the historical sites, this is the place to have lunch. With an accomplished chef husband-wife team, it is fair to expect innovative combinations of ingredients in sandwiches and salads like Bill's Creation or the Apple 'N Things Salad. Though known for their cheesecakes, the chocolate desserts are justifiably tempting. If you are into cake or candy making, supplies are for sale within the restaurant's store. Be sure to check out the area upstairs.

PEPPERONI GRILLE
24 East Main Street
Bloomfield, IN 47424
(812) 384-3934
Open Monday-Saturday for lunch & dinner. Closed Sunday.

While checking out the sites in Southern Indiana, your travels might take you to Bloomfield, the county seat of Greene County. On the square you will find a popular Italian restaurant whose owner spent time in Italy studying the food and the culture. The emphasis is on fresh ingredients to "maximize the simplicity of Italian cuisine." Fresh baked rolls and a salad accompany the entrées, which include all kinds of pasta with either fish, meatballs or chicken covered with a variety of tasty sauces. Smoked salmon ravioli is another mouthwatering choice. Save room for a homemade dessert.

PERILLO'S PIZZERIA

5 South Broadway Street
North Salem, IN 46165
(765) 676-4171
Open Wednesday-Monday for lunch & dinner. Closed Tuesday.
CASH ONLY.

From the outside, Perillo's looks like a little European restaurant with umbrellas and tables on one side and a park on the other. Inside, the story of the restaurant with strong ties to Italy is pictured on the walls. There is an obvious feeling of pride in preparing and serving the family recipes. One customer said, "What makes the pizzas and the calzones the best is the dough!" Pizza can be ordered by the slice with the option of selecting your favorite toppings, and half-orders of pasta dishes are available. For those eating gluten free, cauliflower crust pizzas are a choice. For dessert, there are homemade cannolis and limoncello cake.

PETERSON'S

7690 East 96th Street
Fishers, IN 46038
(317) 598-8863
www.petersonsrestaurant.com
Open Monday-Saturday for dinner. Closed Sunday.

Peterson's boasts "Only the Very Best" and clearly lives up to its commitment. Locally owned by Joe Peterson and his family, the restaurant provides one-of-a-kind steak and seafood entrées in the spirit of regional American cuisine. Maine lobster, Maine diver sea scallops and Atlantic swordfish are outstanding choices. Prime grade steaks and chops are attractively presented on a plate with colorful vegetables. Peterson's has been recognized with an Award of Excellence from the <u>Wine Spectator</u> and also has a nice selection of premium vodkas, malt scotches, and barrel bourbons.The full dinner menu is available in the lounge where live music is featured on weekends.

PIT STOP BARBECUE & GRILL

932 East Main Street
Brownsburg, IN 46112
(317) 858-8370
www.pitstopBBQandgrill.com
Open Monday-Saturday for lunch & dinner; Sunday for brunch.

Some Dining Secret followers may remember the catfish at Frank & Mary's in Pittsboro. Well, when his restaurant closed, Frank gave the staff at Pit Stop his catfish recipe and trained them to duplicate it. Thus, in addition to having award-winning slow smoked barbecue dinner choices, there is Frank & Mary's catfish. The restaurant is filled with a significant amount of 500 memorabilia that creates a race track atmosphere. A large selection of appetizers, sandwiches and sides guarantees something to satisfy everyone. There is also a buffet on Wednesday nights.

PIZZOLOGY PIZZERIA & PUB

13190 Hazel Dell Parkway
Carmel, IN 46033
(317) 844-2550
www.pizzologyindy.com
Open daily for lunch & dinner.

Rarely does one find a pizza restaurant that has an ideology. Pizzology does: "pizza is a balance between crust and ingredients." Their crust is a unique blend of wild yeast, spring water, and Caputo Pizzeria "00" flour. The list of toppings is extensive and even includes a fresh farm egg, wild mushrooms and truffle oil, but the house made cheese and sausage should not be ignored. Once assembled, the pizzas are baked in an 800 degree oven that renders a crispy, yet chewy crust. Soup and salads are offered as sides.

PORT HOLE INN

8939 East South Shore Drive
Lake Lemon (south shore)
Unionville, IN 47468
(812) 339-1856
Open Tuesday-Friday for dinner; Saturday & Sunday for lunch & dinner.
Closed Monday.

This little country tavern sits right off the road, making it an easy stop for people who are in the area and have a taste for juicy catfish, a steak, or perhaps just a sandwich. Popular side dishes to enjoy with the meal include hush puppies, potato cakes and slaw. You can eat in the bar or in the family dining area. Enjoy music on the weekends in season.

POWERS HAMBURGERS

1402 Harrison Street
Fort Wayne, IN 46802
(260) 422-6620
Open Monday-Saturday for breakfast, lunch & dinner.
Closed Sunday.
CASH ONLY.

As you walk across from the courthouse, you see a small white building with striped awnings and you can smell hamburgers and onions cooking. It is not hard to find Powers as nothing much has changed since it opened in 1940. The menu posted on the wall offers breakfast choices plus hamburgers, coney dogs, ham and cheese sandwiches and chips, but no French fries. The sliders are nostalgically referred to as "onion burgers with meat" and draw people from all around. You can sit on a stool at the counter to enjoy your meal.

PRIMO

1326 Broad Street
New Castle, IN 46362
(765) 388-2777
www.primonewcastle.com
Open Wednesday-Friday for lunch & dinner; Saturday for dinner; Sunday for brunch.
Closed Monday & Tuesday.

The sign of a good restaurant is one filled with local residents. Primo boasts a fine dining experience in a comfortable environment. Tables surround a slightly elevated contemporary bar. Walls are filled with large, colorful posters advertising beverages. The spaghetti and meatballs in marinara sauce and lasagna Bolognese are made in-house daily and have their own unique flavor. An alternative might be the chicken bacon mac or a tomato fresca sandwich. There is also a menu for those concerned about gluten.

PROCOPIO'S

127 North Second Street
Vincennes, IN 47591
(812) 882-0914
www.procopiospizzaandpasta.com
Open Tuesday-Friday for lunch & dinner; Saturday & Sunday for dinner.
Closed Monday.

If you ask where there is a good place to eat dinner in Vincennes, Procopio's will most likely be mentioned. A hands-on and homemade image is projected by the owner's presence. There is a pasta special of the day, but you can't go wrong with any entrée that includes the delicious tomato sauce. The pizzas have a great crust and as you dine, you will witness a brisk carry out business as well. Call ahead to find out what night the pre-fix menu is offered as it is a very popular night.

PROVISION

2721 East 86th Street, Suite 200
Indianapolis, IN 46240
(317) 843-6105
www.provision-restaurant.com
Open daily for dinner.

Provision is a place to go as an over-the-top treat to yourself and your guests. The food is well worth the price. The menu changes with the season and ingredients are locally sourced and imaginatively prepared. The surroundings of the Ironworks Hotel also add a very special touch. The setting is hard to explain but contemporary mixed with iron relics will have to do! Outside seating is available. They take pride in their extensive wine list.

PURE EATERY

8235 East 116th Street, Suite 245
Fishers, IN 46038
(317) 288-0285
www.pureeatery.com
Open daily for lunch & dinner. Brunch on Saturday & Sunday.

The promise of this restaurant is "fresh honest food;" in fact, the soups and salad dressings are made from scratch every morning. The menu reflects a lot of imagination with options like gouda-stuffed jalapeños, smoked ham with rosemary aioli, bourbon peanut shrimp wrap, cranberry & goat cheese salad, seared citrus tuna, and a side dish of carrot & cucumber with herbed ranch. Rest assured, there are many tasty choices and the kids' menu includes grilled cheese squares and mac and cheese.

RAIL EPICUREAN MARKET

211 Park Street
Westfield, IN 46074
(317) 450-4981
www.railepicureanmarket.com
Open Tuesday-Saturday for lunch & dinner. Closed Sunday & Monday.

Tucked away on a back street of old Westfield, you will find what looks like a small red barn. As you enter, the aroma of good things cooking is overwhelming. The atmosphere is inviting with a community table and several other places to sit. Shelves of food products created in local kitchens and fresh produce from Hoosier markets surround the eating area. Old sliding doors, light fixtures from an old barn and eager to please staff complete the picture. The menu is presented on a blackboard and often reflects changes as the chef works with the best available products.

RALPH & AVA'S CAFÉ

6 West Main Street
Mooresville, IN 46158
(317) 834-9780
www.ralphandavas.com
Open Tuesday-Saturday for lunch & dinner. Closed Sunday & Monday.

The restaurant's motto is "Be nice or go away." Upon entering the café, you are invited to sit at one of the assorted tables, each with different chairs and most with unique table lamps. Seats are also available at the bar under the "crapelier," a chandelier made of junk. Should you have to wait for a table, there is a jigsaw puzzle up front to keep you busy. The extensive lunch menu includes soups, salads, sandwiches and wraps. Referring to the pretzel melt, a customer raved, "It'll change your life!" The dinner specials change weekly.

RALPH'S GREAT DIVIDE

743 East New York Street
Indianapolis, IN 46202
(317) 637-2192
www.ralphsgreatdivide.com
Open Monday-Friday for lunch; Saturday for dinner. Closed Sunday.

As you walk through the door, your attention is immediately drawn to the walls filled with Indiana history. Sketches, memorabilia, and tributes to family member Ralph are just a few examples. Behind the bar there is an old walk-in cooler dating to the 1930s filled with beer. Beginning with the listing of "unusual hours," the menu is fun to read. Ralph's is known for its "Hot Pot Aug,™" a cream of potato soup au gratin. There's also a "Hot Pot Pig" which adds bacon and hot pepper cheese. A large variety of sandwiches include some with catchy names like the Ethel, the Lucy and the horsey mushroom burger. The club sandwiches are recommended by local law enforcement agencies. A trip to Ralph's is a delightful experience.

RATHSKELLER RESTAURANT

401 East Michigan Street
Indianapolis, IN 46204
(317) 636-0396
www.rathskeller.com
Open daily for lunch & dinner.

Social organizations were an important tradition for early German immigrants in Indianapolis. Thus, in 1894, plans were initiated to build a large club house as a social, cultural, recreational and sports center. Today, this ornate building with its brick facade, slate roof and gables is home to many entertainment and dining events. The Rathskeller feels like an old German beer cellar: the sites, the smells, the food, the beer. Deutsche schnitzel, rouladen, sauerbraten, wurst, and spaetzle are available. The menu offers many other choices as well: seafood, pasta, steak, and vegetarian. Visiting the Rathskeller is both a culinary and historical treat.

RED GERANIUM

520 North Street
New Harmony, IN 47631
(812) 682-4431
www.newharmonyinn.com
Open daily for lunch & dinner. Brunch on weekends.

Established in 1964, the Red Geranium is one of the area's most charming restaurants. Serving breakfast, lunch and dinner, the "Red" offers seasonal American cuisine and midwest favorites. Diners may choose one of three distinctively different dining rooms. The Main Dining Room captures the romance and Old World charm of the nineteenth century. The Green Room offers comfortable benches and a cozy, casual atmosphere. Ornate hand-carved doors grace the entrance to the third room, the Tillich Room (named for philosopher Paul Tillich) and offers a panoramic, pastoral view of a serene lake. At night, the warmth of a large fireplace adds to the romantic setting of this room. The Grapevine Bar serves fine liquors, draft beers, and wines by the glass.

RED WAGON RESTAURANT & BAR
6950 Frontage Road
Poseyville, IN 47633
(812) 874-2221
www.redwagonrestaurant.com
Open daily for breakfast, lunch & dinner.

In one sentence, the Red Wagon serves every category of food in almost every imaginable environment. In an effort to provide the local community with a place to eat, the owners (farmers, hunters, eaters and drinkers) got together and designed a facility reflecting all of their interests. A rotating wheel in front of a huge barn defines the spot. Inside, one dining area is filled with tractors and farm implements. Another has hunters' catches mounted on the walls. Still another has blacksmith tools. Then, there is a sports bar with team memorabilia from St. Louis, Miami and, of course, Poseyville. The breakfast menu carries the usual items, plus a special bowl of biscuits with a choice of three toppings. The lunch and dinner menu has something for everyone. In addition, a lunch buffet and nightly specials are available.

RIZE
2721 East 86th Street, Suite 120
Indianapolis, IN 46240
(317) 843-6101
www.rize-restaurant.com
Open daily for breakfast & lunch

Located in the lower level of the Ironworks hotel on Keystone and 86th Street, Rize offers healthy, tasty food choices. For breakfast, in addition to the traditional "benny" and regular waffles, there are bowls of fresh fruit accompanying yogurt or pudding and potato waffles. For lunch, there are "lunchables:" toasts (fig, salmon, avocado), sandwiches and salads with choices of dressings that include sunflower and maple vinaigrette. They take pride in their creative use of locally grown ingredients.

ROANOKE VILLAGE INN
190 Main (Off U.S. 24 West)
Roanoke, IN 46783
(260) 672-3707
Open daily for lunch & dinner.

Simply "a bar with great food" is how this full service bar and restaurant was described by a Huntington resident. They are best known for the broiled and deep-fried haddock, deep-fried butterflied shrimp, and the popular 16 ounce barbecued pork chop. Additional choices include barbecued ribs, a full line of steaks, and chicken entrées.

ROBERT'S SOUTHFORK RESTAURANT & PUB

105 South Glick Street
Mulberry, IN 46058
(765) 296-2096
www.southforkpub.com
Open Monday-Saturday for lunch & dinner. Closed Sunday.

Picture a corner restaurant where the fishermen stop to have a bite to eat and then gather afterwards to have a drink and review the day's activities. It is on the south fork of the Wildcat Creek System so wildlife is the theme. There is a conglomeration of items on the walls: fishing poles, nets, snowshoes, Outdoor Life and Field & Stream posters, and fishing lures adorn the adjacent bar. The menu has items you would expect, but also has some surprises: smelt, frog legs, and fresh whole catfish. SouthFork enjoys a history of family ownership and lives up to the message on the wall: "The fondest memories are made when gathered around the table."

ROCK-COLA 50'S CAFÉ

5730 Brookville Road
Indianapolis, IN 46219
(317) 357-2233
www.rockcolacafe.com
Open daily for breakfast, lunch & early dinner.

This '50s diner in the midst of Indianapolis factories is a great neighborhood gathering place. You can eat at the counter or in one of the booths. Either place, you will be kept busy looking at all the '50s memorabilia on the walls and ceiling while waiting for your order. All of the meats are handcut and the grilled tenderloin starts about two inches thick. The cook takes a cleaver, has everyone step back, and then pounds it flat right on the grill. The sandwiches are served on fresh bakery buns with a knife sticking straight up, inviting you to cut into them. Hamburgers, veggie burgers, BLT and a Poor Boy's Delite are popular choices, but the Philly is reported to be the best. Of course, there are milkshakes, malts and vanilla, chocolate and lemon cokes. Special breakfast entrées combine eggs with pork chops, ham, steak and bacon. On Saturday, there is a breakfast buffet that offers it all.

ROD AND GUN STEAKHOUSE

2525 East Lambert
Rosedale, IN 47874
(812) 466-2521
Open Friday & Saturday for dinner.

The restaurant dates back to the roaring '20s when, as part of a local farm, it was offered as the stakes in a gambling game. Eleven-year-old Bob Johnson was hired by the new owner and became a very dedicated employee. Over the years there was a fire and then another change in ownership, but in 1975, Bob Johnson did what he thought was impossible: he bought the restaurant, which his son continues to operate today. There are no cards or dice around and the roulette wheel is silent, but the intimate dining areas carry on the tradition and the story. Of course, steaks are the specialty with a 20-ounce porterhouse leading the list. Chicken and seafood are also available.

ROOK CAFÉ

501 Virginia Avenue, #101
Indianapolis, IN 46203
(317) 737-2293
www.rookindy.com
Open Monday-Saturday for lunch & dinner. Closed Sunday.

The setting is sleek and functional with red being the only color that meets the eye until the colorful food arrives. Contemporary Asian street fare is the focus of the flavors presented on a menu that changes with the seasons. For starters, there are steamed buns. Then, you may choose from numerous plates of vegetables, spice, noodles, seafood and assorted meats. Top off your meal with a Halo Halo dessert that brings a smile of satisfaction to the entire taste experience.

ROSIE'S PLACE

88 North 9th Street
Noblesville, IN 46060
(317) 770-3322
www.rosiesplace.net
Open daily for breakfast & lunch.

In addition to the restaurant, Rosie's also features a bakery. As you enter, there is a mouthwatering selection of cakes, pies, cookies and rolls. The seasonal menu and the daily specials continue to activate the senses. For breakfast, there are egg choices that include several different "bennys" (eggs Benedict) and varieties of pancakes. Lunch sandwiches on the bakery's homemade breads are accompanied by a side or a cup of soup. The salad selections have tasty combinations of ingredients. Don't forget about the desserts at the entrance. Rosie's is also sensitive to the gluten-free needs of patrons.

RUSTED SILO SOUTHERN BBQ & BREWHOUSE

411 North State Street (Hwy 39)
Lizton, IN 46149
(317) 994-6145
www.rustedsilobrewhouse.com
Open Monday-Saturday for lunch & dinner. Closed Sunday.

A visit to the Rusted Silo is an experience. It is on the main highway but not easy to find as it is a small shack that sits between a used car lot and the railroad tracks. Open the door and find a wall of floor-to-ceiling coolers on one side, a few tables on the other. There is a lot of noise and a huge amount of heat coming off the open pit oven loaded with meats and poultry. The pit master is carefully carving and preparing the food that has been ordered at the counter. Pork butt, smoked chicken, brisket and spareribs are the menu choices, along with southern sides of collards, cheese grits, coleslaw and corn on the cob. The food is "finger-licking" good and well worth taking the step inside. Mama June's Nanna pudding can complete the meal.

RUSTY DOG IRISH PUB

32 North Jefferson
Huntington, IN 46750
(260) 579-0433
www.rustydogirishpub.com
Open Tuesday-Saturday for dinner. Closed Sunday & Monday.

A rusty dog hanging over the door marks the spot. Along with the commanding bar and wooden tables, the dark green walls decorated with pictures of hunting dogs transport you to Ireland. The menu reflects an Irish theme with items like cheddar potato soup, bangers and mash, grilled cod Kinsale, and, of course, Guiness hot mustard. There are also sandwich baskets named after different breeds of dogs. The dinner menu offers the standard fare of ribeye steak and smoked pork loin chop, but there is also Shepherd's Pie and Haddock Oscar. On the whole, the menu reflects a lot of imagination.

RUTH'S KEYSTONE CAFÉ

3443 East 86th Street
Indianapolis, IN 46240
(317) 757-8006
www.ruthscafeindy.com
Open daily for breakfast & lunch.

Many patterns and colors grab the eye as you enter the café. Each chair is a different color, some with curliques, but no two are the same. Look to the blackboard for the day's special offerings: omelets, quiches, soups, salads and sandwiches. Each item has a unique combination of ingredients and taste treats. There's also an extensive menu with a Norwegian choice worth trying: Norwegian lefses, which are rolled potato cakes with butter, cinnamon and sugar, or possibly strawberries. Ruth's serves breakfast all day, every day and promises a lunch that is fresh and local.

ST. ELMO STEAK HOUSE

127 South Illinois Street
Indianapolis, IN 46225
(317) 635-0636
www.stelmos.com
Open daily for dinner.

St. Elmo's is no secret to diners, but it must be included in any local restaurant guide as an Indianapolis institution with a national reputation. A downtown landmark since 1902, it is considered the oldest Indianapolis steak house in the same location. Many celebrities, rock stars, professional athletes, and politicians have dined here when in town. If you are craving an exceptional steak, this is the place to treat yourself to one. But you can't dine at St. Elmo's without ordering their signature shrimp cocktail with fiery horseradish cocktail sauce, the most popular and well-known item on the menu. The excellent food, ambiance, professional service and history all combine to create an exceptional dining experience.

ST. JAMES RESTAURANT
204 East Albion Street
Avilla, IN 46710
(260) 897-2114
www.stjamesavilla.com
Open Monday-Saturday for breakfast, lunch & dinner. Closed Sunday.

The Indiana Restaurant Association recognized the St. James as the oldest restaurant in Northern Indiana, named after the James family who built the original hotel in 1878. The Freeman family refurbished the deteriorated hotel in 1948 and continued to remodel, making it the successful dining establishment it is today. The history of the building is documented in photographs displayed throughout. St. James' broasted chicken tops the menu, but there are steaks, seafood, pork dinners and sandwiches as well. There are also some sinful desserts like Snickers pie, totally turtle cheesecake, and freshly baked pies. A full bar is available with your favorite beverages.

ST. JOSEPH BREWERY & PUBLIC HOUSE
540 North College Avenue
Indianapolis, IN 46202
(317) 602.5670
Open Tuesday-Sunday for lunch & dinner; Sunday brunch. Closed Monday.

Originally the fourth catholic church established in Indianapolis, the 135-year-old building has been uniquely renovated into a restaurant/brewpub. The no-frills interior has an open dining area surrounded by arches and tall windows. Church pews provide seating in the waiting area. The shiny brewing tanks are housed on what was once the church altar. The food is a step up from the typical brewpub fare, starting with a nice selection of appetizers, soups and salads. A large variety of sandwiches and entrées fill the menu. The bar is a busy spot where patrons sample some of the appropriately-named craft brews, like "Holy Rolled Oats." The choir loft has been converted into a private dining area for larger groups or parties.

SAHM'S ALE HOUSE
VILLAGE OF WEST CLAY
12819 East New Market Street
Carmel, IN 46032
(317) 853-6278
www.sahmsalehouse.com
Open daily for lunch & dinner.

Sahm's restaurants are located throughout Indianapolis. However, this Ale House is located in the unique community of West Clay, where a small village has been built around shops and public meeting spaces. The focus of this Sahm's is on wood-fired pizza offered in the evening, but if time is not a problem, you most likely can order it at lunchtime. Typical menu items are offered, but there are exceptions like Tatchos (loaded tatter tots) or a Clint Eastwood hamburger. Salads can be ordered as large or small and tacos have many combinations. The Bulgogi bowl is an unusual favorite of one diner. For dinner, there is meatloaf, salmon, pork chops and steak. Most of the entrées offer sides and there are at least 20 different choices.

SAIGON RESTAURANT
4760 West 38th Street
Indianapolis, IN 46254
(317) 927-7270
www.saigonrestaurant-indy.com
Open Wednesday-Monday for lunch & dinner. Closed Tuesday.

At first the menu is overwhelming, but soon the diner recognizes the nice variety of soups, salads, assorted noodles and rice dishes. Then, there is beef, seafood, chicken, pork and vegetable choices. A look at the freshly cooked foods delivered to surrounding tables whets the appetite. It is up to you to decide the combination and the spiciness you desire. Vietnamese specialties are offered along with Oriental favorites. A unique extra is the Crazy Bubble Tea, a frothy, icy tapioca drink served with a thick straw. It is hard to believe that something so tasty is healthy. You will be surprised by the inviting atmosphere in this restaurant.

SAKURA RESTAURANT
7201 North Keystone Avenue
Indianapolis, IN 46240
(317) 259-4171
www.indysakura.com
Open Tuesday-Saturday for lunch & dinner; Sunday for dinner. Closed Monday.

Sakura was one of the first restaurants to introduce many Indianapolis residents to the sushi concept. The parking lot around this white house is always full at lunch or dinner time—a sign of good food. You can sit and watch the sushi being made or take a booth. For lunch, boxes offer different combinations of rolls, tempura, sushi and sashimi. Sushi can be ordered a la carte as nigiri (fish topped rice), rolls or a combination. Soba (gray buckwheat pasta) or udon (thick white soft wheat) noodles and donburi (rice bowls) are available, as well as a number of Japanese dinners.

SANDRA D'S ITALIAN GARDEN
1330 South Main Street
Auburn, IN 46706
(260) 927-7282
www.sandradsitaliangarden.com
Open Wednesday-Saturday for lunch & dinner; Sunday for lunch.

While visiting the outlet mall in northern Indiana, go into the town of Auburn and look for the café awning at the end of Main Street. Your hostess is Sandra Dillinger and her husband, Bentley, is the chef. The cuisine is authentic Italian. The menu includes traditional pasta dishes, but worthy of mention are some unique items: crispy ravioli antipasti, carne panini with the chef's homemade rosemary flat bread, Sandra D's original chicken crepes, apple pizza, beef tenderloin rosa, and salmon griglia. This quaint café offers a pleasant respite for the shopper or traveler.

SAWASDEE

122 West 86th Street
Indianapolis, IN 46260
(317) 844-9451
www.sawasdeeindy.com
Open Monday-Saturday for lunch & dinner; Sunday for dinner.

Thai food has become very popular and Mr. Ty's family has been educating the Sawasdee patrons for years. The menu has pictures and good descriptions, but there is always someone available to help the inexperienced figure out what to order and how spicy to make the dish. Soup and a spring roll or Thai salad are served with all of the entrées. The curry dishes are very special but you may select the old standby noodle dish called Pad Thai. There are also soups, stir frys and rice dishes. At the end of your meal, you are given a slice of orange to sweeten your palate. With glass table tops, fresh flowers and eager-to-please servers, Sawasdee (meaning "hello, how are you?") is a restaurant that sparkles.

SCHNITZELBANK RESTAURANT

393 Third Avenue
Jasper, IN 47546
(812) 482-2640
www.schnitzelbankrestaurant.com
Open Monday-Saturday for breakfast, lunch & dinner. Closed Sunday.

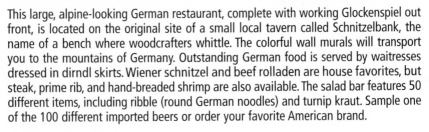

This large, alpine-looking German restaurant, complete with working Glockenspiel out front, is located on the original site of a small local tavern called Schnitzelbank, the name of a bench where woodcrafters whittle. The colorful wall murals will transport you to the mountains of Germany. Outstanding German food is served by waitresses dressed in dirndl skirts. Wiener schnitzel and beef rolladen are house favorites, but steak, prime rib, and hand-breaded shrimp are also available. The salad bar features 50 different items, including ribble (round German noodles) and turnip kraut. Sample one of the 100 different imported beers or order your favorite American brand.

SCHOLARS KEEP

717 North College Avenue
Bloomington, IN 47404
(812) 332-1892
www.scholarskeep.com
Open daily for dinner & Sunday for brunch.

Scholars Keep is housed in a nearly 200-year-old mansion with a lot of history. In fact, the lower level (now the wine cellar) was once connected to the underground railroad. The first floor is a casual gathering spot with a wall of chalkboard behind the newly renovated 18-seat bar. Seating is also available upstairs in the more quiet, intimate dining room. The list of dinner appetizers is extensive and includes unique items like lamb lollipops and eggplant caponata. There are salads, tasty soups, and variations of burgers and flatbreads for a lighter meal. Full dinner entrees include steaks, salmon, roasted vegetable risotto, and the popular lemon-thyme chicken.

SHALLOS ANTIQUE RESTAURANT & BREWHOUSE
8811 Hardegan Street (County Line Mall)
Indianapolis, IN 46227
(317) 882-7997
www.shallos.com
Open daily for lunch & dinner.

A variety of beers and an eclectic mix of local memorabilia are what draws people to Shallos, which proudly claims to be "the midwest's largest purveyor of rare and exotic beers!" There are over 500 beer choices—40 on draft, both imported and microbrewed. A collection of bottles and at least 300 tap handles border the upstairs and downstairs walls, accented with pictures of significance to Hoosiers. The menu cover carries out the antique theme when it boldly advertises "Air Conditioned and Ice Water!" A variety of appetizers and sandwiches fills the menu, along with full dinner entrées. Try your main course "swamped," a Caribbean marinade specialty.

SHAPIRO'S DELICATESSEN
808 South Meridian Street
Indianapolis, IN 46225
(317) 631-4041
www.shapiros.com
Open daily for breakfast, lunch & dinner.

Established in 1905, Shapiro's is now in its fourth generation of ownership. Today's staff continues to treat every day as if it were opening day, as witnessed by those going through the line and seeing the enthusiasm of the servers. There is often a moment of panic when you see all the tantalizing choices. The desserts come first and the pies, baked in-house, are almost impossible to pass by. The sandwiches are next: corned beef, pastrami, peppered beef, brisket, summer sausage, and chopped liver, all served on rye bread or egg bun with or without a dill pickle. If you get by that station, you can choose one of the plate meals: stuffed pepper or cabbage, beef burger with grilled onions, meat loaf or chicken. The complete meal comes with two sides: macaroni and cheese, baked beans, green beans or noodles. At this point, you take a deep breath, sit down at one of the many tables, and savor every delicious bite.

SHOEFLY PUBLIC HOUSE
122 East 22nd Street
Indianapolis, IN 46202
(317) 283-5007
www.shoeflypublichouse.com
Open Monday-Saturday for lunch & dinner. Closed Sunday.

There isn't a story behind the Shoefly name, but there is good reason to visit this neighborhood gathering spot. The goal is to use locally grown food to prepare "approachable pub food." For starters, try the hummus on a large crisp shell. Next, choose from pretzel flatbreads with uniquely creative toppings, sandwiches like the Cuban pork and smoked gouda, or walleye tacos, to name a few options. The "no meatloaf" melt and "whatever" burger choices make you smile. Full plate entrées are also on the menu. The public house has locally crafted beverages available.

SIMMONS WINERY & 450 NORTH BREWING CO.

8111 East 450 North
Columbus, IN 47203
(812) 546-0091
www.simmonswinery.com, www.450northbrewing.com
Open daily for lunch & dinner.

Catering to the wine drinkers' beer drinking friends, the Simmons family created one of the first winery and brewery operations in Indiana. Handcrafted beers and a variety of wines are made at this 131-year-old farm outside Columbus. You can sip your drink sitting on a keg at the bar or at a table. Brick oven pizza is on the menu and can be ordered by the slice. The crust is crisp and ingredients carefully selected. The menu also includes choices from a garlic knot appetizer to a sugar coated twisted pizza dough dessert with an assortment of options in between: salads, sandwiches and pasta.

SLEEPY OWL SUPPER CLUB

11374 North State Road 13
Syracuse, IN 46567
(574) 457-4840
www.sleepyowlrestaurant.com
Open daily for lunch & dinner.

There is a sleepy owl on a branch over the door but lots of activity inside. The menu lists many familiar choices packaged in a different way, such as armadillo eggs (stuffed jalepeno peppers) and foot o'rings (onion rings with warrior sauce). The "Pasta Picks" are Italian dishes from the recipes of the owner's grandmother. The homemade breaded tenderloin made the Sleepy Owl famous—it is so big, it won't fit in the bun! An "endless bowl of salad" accompanies the entrées of steak, chicken, pork chops, and barbecued ribs. The "World's Smallest Sundae" for 50 cents is a "sweet ending."

SLIPPERY NOODLE INN

372 South Meridian Street
Indianapolis, IN 46225
(317) 631-6974
www.slipperynoodle.com
Open Monday-Saturday for lunch & dinner;
Sunday for dinner.

The Slippery Noodle has quite a colorful history both above and below the ground. Established in 1850, it is listed in the National Register of Historic Places and is believed to be the oldest commercial building left standing in Indianapolis. Located close to the train station, it was originally built as a road house and bar for railroad passengers, became a way station for the Underground Railroad during the Civil War, and even housed a bordello which operated until 1953. Today, the live blues bands featured seven nights a week are the Noodle's claim to fame. Patrons enjoy grabbing a bite to eat from a variety of sandwich, sub, snack, and dinner choices while listening to music and absorbing the history of this Indiana landmark.

SO BRO CAFÉ
653 East 52nd Street
Indianapolis, IN 46205
(317) 920-8121
www.sobrocafe.com
Open daily for lunch & dinner; Saturday & Sunday for brunch.

This small, welcoming café offers a healthy meal, creatively prepared with natural and local foods. Its location in a neighborhood where people walk to restaurants creates a comfortable and friendly community atmosphere. The meals are prepared with delightful combinations of tastes: garden Maki rolls, curried lentils, blackened organic tofu, or salmon with lemon dill sauce. While tempeh, quinoa and kale appear several times on the menu, you may also select a bison burger, 52nd Street Salad or chicken cordon blue.

SOME GUYS PIZZA-PASTA-GRILL
6235 Allisonville Road
Indianapolis, IN 46220
(317) 257-1364
Open Tuesday-Friday for lunch & dinner;
Saturday & Sunday for dinner. Closed Monday.

A neighborhood gathering place for years, Some Guys is a comfortable family spot that has withstood the test of time. Bruce Dean's expression of "Some Guys...it's an art" is presented in paintings and murals that decorate the walls of each booth. Wood-fired pizza got its start here in Indianapolis with Santa Fe, Jamaican, BBQ chicken and Greek pizza among the specialties. You can design your own pizza or choose the traditional or vegetarian. For those who are not pizza hungry, there are salads, woodoven pasta dishes and sandwiches. The first weekend of the month is "Lasagna Weekend."

SOUTH SIDE SODA SHOP
1122 South Main Street
Goshen, IN 46526
(574) 534-3790
www.southsidesodashopdiner.com
Open Tuesday-Saturday for lunch & dinner. Closed Sunday & Monday.

Originally opened in 1910 as a grocery store, this establishment became a soda shop in 1940 and the restaurant was added in 1990. Located on a point in the road, you could almost run into the Soda Shop as you drive down Main Street. It is a treat to enter through the bakery where pies of the day, chosen from over 40 varieties, are on display. Seating is available in the old black and white soda bar with booths, or at the tables up front with a pleasant outside view. You may be tempted to eat dessert first from the list of many traditional handmade ice cream and fountain specialties. There are sandwiches, Philly hoagies, salads and daily soup specials for lunch. Supper at the Soda Shop includes seafood, pasta and chicken options.

SPOKE & STEELE

123 South Illinois Street
Indianapolis, IN 46225
(317) 737-1616
www.spokeandsteele.com
Open daily for breakfast, lunch & dinner.

This neighborhood-style restaurant is located on the ground floor of a boutique hotel, Le Meridien. Large picture windows offer great views where you can take in the sites of downtown Indianapolis. Led by a James Beard nominated chef, Spoke & Steele focuses on quality food and drinks designed around locally-sourced ingredients. Enjoy a craft cocktail and charcuterie board in the modern, yet cozy, lounge or order the signature Spoke Burger in the main restaurant. Whether ordering off the breakfast, lunch or dinner menu, you won't be disappointed in the meal or the surroundings.

STABLES STEAKHOUSE

939 Poplar Street
Terre Haute, IN 47807
(812) 232-6677
www.stablessteakhouse.com
Open daily for dinner.

The warm and inviting atmosphere of this restaurant creates the feeling that you are in a casual, well-renovated historic setting. Built in 1890 as a stable for the brewery across the street, the look has been preserved throughout the interior. There are horse stalls, high ceilings, barn accessories, and horses decorating the furniture upholstery. The main fare is hand-cut steaks, but the menu also includes a one pound pork chop, chicken, fresh seafood, lobster and pasta. A wine cellar and well-stocked bar is available for your enjoyment. Banquet facilities and catering are available.

STONE HEARTH CAFÉ

2131 North Centerville Road
Centerville, IN 47330
(765) 855-2000
www.outletstore.warmglow.com
Open daily for lunch & early dinner (closes at 5 pm).

There is more than one reason to stop at the Warm Glow Outlet Store on Interstate 70: shop, eat or combine the two. You will enjoy browsing through a huge assortment of candle, specialty gift items and food products. The adjacent Watering Can houses a farmers market and garden center. The Stone Hearth Cafe was added at this site to provide shoppers with a bite to eat. They take pride in the Jo Jo Martin's BBQ pork and brisket, which is smoked daily. Stone hearth pizzas and specialty sandwiches are also offered. If it is later in the day, you might want to treat yourself to a piece of pie, cobbler or some of the hand-dipped ice creams.

STONE HOUSE RESTAURANT & BAKERY
124 East Main Street
Delphi, IN 46923
(765) 564-4663
Open Monday-Saturday for breakfast, lunch & dinner. Closed Sunday.

This historic building opened as a saloon and brothel in 1874 and continued to house a bar until the 1980s. Today, you'll find a small town, downtown restaurant offering not only breakfast, lunch and dinner, but a bakery filled with homemade breads, pies, cookies and muffins. Breakfast egg dishes are accompanied by a giant cinnamon roll as a side, or you might prefer the cinnamon bread French toast. Lunch choices include hamburgers, grilled or breaded tenderloin and various chicken sandwiches, served with chips and a pickle. Dinner selections include ham steak with grilled pineapple, rib eye steak and fried chicken. They invite you to "stop in for real home cookin' today!"

STOOKEY'S
125 East Main Street
Thorntown, IN 46071
(765) 436-7202
www.stookeys.com
Open Tuesday-Saturday for lunch & dinner. Closed Sunday & Monday.

If you mention catfish to <u>Dining Secrets</u> readers, many will respond, "Have you been to Stookey's?" In the small town of Thorntown, just northwest of Indianapolis, you will find great catfish, a tasty ribeye steak, and "out-of-this-world" onion rings. The Stookey family opened and operated the restaurant starting in 1975. The current owners are committed to the Stookey name and are dedicated to upholding the restaurant's fine reputation. Race fans will appreciate the "500" decor in the bar.

STORY INN
6404 South State Road 135
Story, IN 47448
(812) 988-2273
www.storyinn.com
Open Tuesday-Sunday for brunch & dinner.
Closed Monday. Reservations requested for dinner.

Located in a village representative of a rural 19th century trading community, this charming country inn is a fun retreat for dinner after a day in Brown County or an athletic event at I.U. The main floor of the General Store is virtually unaltered and houses the gourmet restaurant. The menu features cuisine that is prepared in-house from fresh, local seasonal ingredients, along with award-winning desserts and appetizers. Bed and Breakfast rooms are available upstairs and in surrounding cottages. The ultimate Story experience is dining on the screened porch during a heavy rain and hearing the raindrops fall on the tin roof.

STREAMLINER

201 East 9th Street
Rochester, IN 46975
(574) 223-4656
www.streamlinerrestaurant.com
Open daily for lunch & dinner.

The Streamliner has been a local institution for over 75 years and housed in its current location for over 30 years. An assortment of antiques is displayed at the entrance. Loyal and knowledgeable servers can familiarize you with the history. It is conveniently located as you travel north or south through Indiana on U.S. 31. There is even a drive-up window so orders can be called in and picked up. The restaurant is famous for its tenderloins but also offers hamburgers, sandwiches, steaks, fish, and salads, freshly made with organic ingredients. There are some interesting specialty items, including breaded green beans and sweet potato fries with marshmallow cream dip.

SUNNY ITALY CAFÉ

601 North Niles Avenue
South Bend, IN 46616
(574) 232-9620
www.sunnyitalycafe.com
Open Wednesday-Saturday for dinner. Closed Sunday-Tuesday.

Located in a downtown neighborhood once known as "Little Italy," this family-owned establishment is reported to be South Bend's oldest Italian restaurant. The philosophy is that customers should be treated like family, and that is the feeling you get when you dine here. Their spaghetti is famous, along with a nice variety of other pasta dishes, all made from generations-old recipes. The menu also includes steaks, chops and seafood. Family-style dinners (for 15 people or more) are very popular and include spaghetti, ravioli, chicken cacciatore and fried or broiled chicken. This is a nice option for large parties and celebrations.

TABLE by MARKET DISTRICT

11505 North Illinois
Carmel, IN 46032
(317) 689-6330
www.marketdistrict.com
Open daily for lunch & dinner. Brunch on Sunday.

The charm of this unique setting is that it is located in a huge grocery store. Diners know they are eating the freshest food and after their meal, can shop the extensive inventory at the Market District store. The menu offers appetizers, sandwiches, salads, and full dinners. Sunday's brunch includes biscuits and gravy, chicken and waffles, and also a Jack Benny that is a seafood cake sandwich. Kids are encouraged to "become foodies" by offering small portions of regular menu items in addition to a menu of kid favorites.

TAMALE PLACE

5226 Rockville Road
Indianapolis, IN 46224
(317) 248-9771
www.thetamaleplace.com
Open Monday-Saturday for breakfast, lunch & dinner; Sunday for lunch & dinner.

If you are seeking authentic tamales, this is the place to go. Handmade with corn dough processed in the original Mexican way, these tamales are good and are advertised as weighing in at about one-half pound. Tacos, tortas and nachos are offered with a variety of toppings, including fresh cilantro and pickled jalapenos. Pozole, a cold weather thick soup, is offered seasonally. Whether you dine in or carry out, you will think you are eating food made in Acapulco.

TASTE CAFÉ & MARKETPLACE

5164 North College Avenue
Indianapolis, IN 46205
(317) 925-2233
www.tastecafeandmarketplace.com
Open daily for breakfast & lunch;
Wednesday & Thursday for dinner.

Creative combinations of ingredients make dining at Taste a pleasurable experience. Imagine breakfast choices that include a granola parfait, or a "c.b.&g.," which is cheddar, biscuits and gravy. For lunch, a mouthwatering array of wonderfully colorful and tasty salads are displayed in the food cases. Pick a salad or two, a sandwich like curried chicken salad, B.A.L.T. (where "A" is for avocado), or roast turkey and smoked bacon. Once you have had a side of french fries, you will come back for more. Desserts abound: hummingbird cake, bread pudding, chocolate cupcakes and more. It is truly a "taste" treat to dine at this restaurant.

TAVERN ON SOUTH

423 West South Street
Indianapolis, IN 46225
(317) 602-3115
www.tavernonsouth.com
Open Monday-Saturday for lunch & dinner. Closed Sunday.

Located in the shadow of Lucas Oil Stadium, this two-story brick structure built in 1910 houses a bar and several dining rooms: upstairs, downstairs, inside and outside. They advertise themselves as being a "casual, yet sophisticated restaurant with a menu focused on seasonally inspired selections utilizing fresh quality ingredients." All of this is true. Salads are served as sides or entrées. In addition, there are sandwiches, pizzas, pastas, and beef, chicken, pork and seafood entrées. The wine and beer menu is extensive and the signature cocktail list is very creative.

T-BERRY'S DINER
501 Lincolnway
LaPorte, IN 46350
(219) 362-6261
www.tberrysdiner.com
Open Monday-Saturday for lunch & dinner. Sunday for lunch.

The brothers Thornberry, David & Don, have created "smashburgers," beef patties with multiple toppings and sauces, or you might enjoy one of the highly touted daily specials. Almost everything served is homemade: noodles, applesauce, slaw, salad dressings, sauces, etc. Each sandwich is unique and can be accompanied by a cup of homemade chicken and noodles. Reportedly, grandma rolls out the noodles everyday. Hot dogs and LaPorte Polish sausage are always on the menu, and grilled perogies are offered on Sunday. A green river float, an old time favorite, is also available.

TC'S RESTAURANT & TAVERN
109 North Railroad Street
Battle Ground, IN 47920
(765) 567-2838
Open Monday-Friday for lunch & dinner; Saturday for dinner.
Closed Sunday.

If you are visiting Wolf Park or nearby Purdue University, TC's Restaurant would be a convenient stop for a bite to eat. Typical tavern food of appetizers and sandwiches is available, but the catfish, smoked pork chops or country ribs might be more to your liking. Thursdays are popular for the prime rib, served with a very special cheese-stuffed potato.

TEGRY BISTRO
6010 West 86th Street, #140
Indianapolis, IN 46278
(317) 802-7848
www.tegrybistro.com
Open Tuesday-Sunday for lunch & dinner. Closed Monday.

You will be pleasantly surprised when you walk in the door of this Trader's Point Shopping Plaza restaurant. The dark wood walls and booths provide an inviting and cozy "fine dining" atmosphere. Attractive Asian "artifacts" decorate the walls. Friendly and well-informed servers answer questions and explain the Asian inspired menu: Nigiri (rice wrapped seafood), Sashimi (chunks of seafood), Maki rolls with seaweed or rice. If sushi is not your choice, there are bento boxes, fried rice and noodle dishes, and the house specials are always tempting.

TEIBEL'S RESTAURANT

1775 U.S. Highway 41 (U.S. 30 & 41)
Schererville, IN 46375
(219) 865-2000
www.teibels.com
Open daily for lunch & dinner.

Teibel's first opened its doors in 1929 and has operated continuously ever since. Their growth continues with a beautifully renovated formal dining room and the addition of a café with a more casual atmosphere. Customers come here for the delicious chicken and lake perch that have made Teibel's famous throughout the area. In fact, the family who submitted this recommendation said they have yet to find any other place where lake perch can compare to Teibel's. Banquet facilities are also available for business meetings or any occasion. Call for banquet menu information.

THAI ORCHID

8145 Bash Street
Indianapolis, IN 46250
(317) 578-8155
www.thaiorchidindy.com
Open daily for lunch & dinner.

The restaurant promises that a "warm and charming atmosphere will instantly relax you while our attentive staff spoils you," which is an appealing thought when traveling to or from the Castleton Square Mall. There are a number of Thai food choices on the lunch menu, each including a salad, spring roll and wonton. For dinner, Traditional Entrées, Signature Curries and Chef's Creations are highlighted on a menu that well describes the numerous rice and noodle dishes.The Thai Orchid is authentic Thai cuisine and asks the diner to specify a spiciness preference, which includes hot, extra hot and Thai hot.

THAI SMILE 2

2401 North Tillotson Avenue
Muncie, IN 47304
(765) 730-0645
Open Monday-Saturday for lunch & dinner. Closed Sunday.

Located across the street from the Ball State University football stadium, this restaurant is easy to find. It is also easy to enjoy the many Thai entrees. The Mongolian BBQ and sesame chicken are recommended, but there is a variety of sushi, noodle, rice, curry, and soup suggestions as well. Dessert is an extra treat! A "sleeping banana" or Thai custard are good choices, but a unique Thai ice cream has been introduced and hopefully catches on. Ingredients of your choice are mashed on a frozen pan and then rolled together, to be consumed with delight.

THE IRISH LION®

212 West Kirkwood
Bloomington, IN 47404
(812) 336-9076
www.irishlion.com
Open daily for lunch & dinner

This long, narrow tavern has been serving food and drink since 1882. The ice house out back, turn-of-the-century metal ceiling, and many antiques decorating the interior are all reminders of its earlier days. In Ireland, where no one point is more than 70 miles from the sea, a lot of seafood is consumed. Thus, after the customary drink to begin the meal, appetizers of shrimp, fresh oysters, mussels, clams, oysters Rockefeller (an original recipe), or Blarney puff balls are offered. For the main course, choose the corned beef and cabbage, Celtic stew, rack of lamb, prime rib, lobster tail, or perhaps the "rineanna"—duckling half with apple-fennel bread stuffing. Top off your meal with a piece of apple walnut cake or whiskey pie.

THE SHERMAN

35 South Main Street
Batesville, IN 47006
(812) 934-1000
www.the-sherman.com
Open Monday-Saturday for breakfast, lunch & dinner. Sunday for brunch & dinner.

Many remember the historic Sherman House, renamed The Sherman, with its history dating back to 1852. Even though there have been renovations and updates made to the old hotel, visitors can still connect with the past. The Black Forest Bar is a focal point and the modern decor highlights memorabilia from old Germany. The dining room has been refurbished but the heavy rich wooden beams and supports are still present. The pictures on the walls document The Sherman's history. Traditional German foods are offered, but American dishes are featured as well.

THREE CARROTS

920 Virginia Avenue
Indianapolis, IN 46203
(463) 221-3669
www.threecarrotsindy.com
Open daily for lunch & dinner. Brunch on Saturday & Sunday.

As you enter the restaurant, a refreshing and healthy feeling permeates the functional contemporary space. Everything you see seems to have a purpose, and that includes the food. The menu advertises "Vegetarian Cuisine from the Heartland." The word "tasty" needs to be inserted as well. Entrees are built around tofu, seitan (gluten bacon) and cauliflower steaks. Loads of vegetables, rice and spice add texture and flavor. There are also familiar sounding items served with a vegan twist: hummus, tacos, kale salad, mac and cheese. The staff happily assists with making selections.

TIMBUKTOO'S

215 East State Road 120
Fremont, IN 46703
(260) 495-1658
www.timbuktoos.com
Open Monday-Saturday for lunch & dinner. Closed Sunday.

Located near Pokagon State Parkl, this charming restaurant is the perfect stop after a day at the Park or when you need a break from cooking. Using the freshest ingredients available, the seasonal menu is filled with a tempting array of appetizers (try the yam fries or spinach balls for something different), specialty salads with homemade dressings, and a nice variety of sandwiches. Creatively prepared entrées, including their award-winning coffee crusted ribeye, feature seafood, chicken, beef and pasta dishes, all very reasonably priced. Make sure you save room for the homemade desserts.

TIPPECANOE PLACE

620 West Washington
South Bend, IN 46601
(574) 234-9077
www.tippe.com
Open Tuesday-Saturday for lunch & dinner;
Sunday for brunch & dinner. Closed Monday.

This elegant mansion, the original home built by the Studebaker family in 1888, is the embodiment of everything great wealth in the 1880s could suggest. Its four levels of exquisite architecture and detailing, including 40 rooms and 20 fireplaces, provided a magnificent backdrop for many lavish events that were prized invitations by South Bend society. Today, Tippecanoe Place is still known for its hospitality and gracious setting for fine dining. With the exception of the modern kitchen and bar, great attention has been paid to preserving these grand rooms that are now the dining areas. Award-winning fare includes a wonderful variety of appetizers, entrées and desserts prepared by the pastry chef. The house specialty is "perfect" prime rib. Sunday brunch is a veritable feast, offering many appealing selections. Reservations are recommended.

TOAST CAFÉ

28 East 13th Street
Anderson, IN 46016
(765) 644-8131
Open daily for breakfast & lunch.

Waitstaff with tee shirts saying, "Get Toasted" or "Got Toast?" welcomes customers to this 60-year-old, family-owned diner. Breakfast is served anytime with "light" or "hearty" early bird specials. The regular menu also includes eggs with five strips of bacon. In addition to sandwiches for lunch, there are four varieties of Manhattans available: roast beef, ground round, and breaded or grilled tenderloin. A blackboard lists the daily specials, which always include the tasty homemade bakery items.

TOP NOTCH BAR & GRILL

113 East 3rd Street
Brookston, IN 47923
(765) 563-6508
www.topnotchbar.com
Open Monday-Friday for lunch & dinner; Saturday for dinner. Closed Sunday.
CASH AND CHECKS ONLY.

Come with a big appetite on Friday and Saturday nights for "Great Steaks, No Bull." Customers rave that the filet mignon is the best at "a price you can't beat!" The atmosphere is casual and friendly where the bartender jokes with patrons and the owners are in the kitchen cooking the steaks and hand-dipping the most flavor-filled onion rings anywhere. Weekday sandwiches are a treat, especially the hand-dipped, freshly cut pork tenderloins. The owners and staff take pride in their establishment and are eager to please their guests. It is a bar, so you must be 21 to enter.

TRE BICCHIERI

425 Washington Street
Columbus, IN 47201
(812) 372-1962
www.trebicchieri-columbus.com
Open Monday-Friday for lunch & dinner; Saturday for dinner. Closed Sunday.

An invitation on the doorway to "enter as strangers, leave as friends" gives you a good indication of how well you will be treated at this downtown restaurant. Tre Bicchieri ("three glasses" in Italian) is the story of three friends who combined their resources to make a dream come true. The menu covers the classic Italian dishes to some innovative entrées. With a French-trained chef in the kitchen, some of the main entrées have some French inspiration. The desserts are made by the owner, and her tiramisu has been talked about in publications nationwide. The Chef's Table can be reserved, a cozy spot separate from the main restaurant with a view of the chefs in action. Be sure to look at the mural painted by local artist Nick Woolls.

TRIPLE XXX RESTAURANT

2 North Salisbury Street
West Lafayette, IN 47906
(765) 743-5373
www.triplexxxfamilyrestaurant.com
Open daily for breakfast, lunch & dinner.
CASH ONLY ESTABLISHMENT.

When a restaurant has been around for over 80 years, it is worth a visit. The literature says "our name may be XXX, but our food is rated G." Burgers are called "chop steaks," 100% sirloin and always fresh, never frozen. They make their own pork BBQ, grilled tenderloins, chili and potato salad. Then there is the root beer: Triple XXX, one of a few independent brands left. The story actually began in a Galveston, Texas, brewery in 1895 and the timeline moves from beer to soft drinks to Triple XXX "thirst stations" (root beer drive-ins). In the restaurant, the root beer is served in a frosty glass or in a float. Bottles can be purchased to take home.

TROJAN HORSE

100 East Kirkwood Avenue (Walnut Street)
Bloomington, IN 47408
(812) 332-1101
www.thetrojanhorse.com
Open daily for lunch & dinner.

As you approach the Trojan Horse, the "public view" kitchen entices passers-by to watch the lamb and beef being carved on the spit for the famous gyros. Inside, there is an I.U. flag and a Greek flag, suggesting that the menu is divided "Greek" and "American." Wonderful Greek appetizers include saganaki (flaming cheese) and dolmas (grape leaves), while the American choices feature super fries, breaded dill pickles and mixed veggies. In addition to gyros, souvlaki (marinated pork and fixings in a pita), a pita melt or tenderloin are offered. Zeus's recommendations for dinner include moussaka and other Greek specialties. If you're feeling indulgent, order the baklava ice cream or ambrosia for dessert. Visit the Hero's Club Bar upstairs and look for the Medusa and Poseidon frescoes left over from the old nautical-themed restaurant.

TRUFFLES RESTAURANT

1131 South College Mall Road
Bloomington, IN 47401
(812) 330-1111
www.trufflesbloomington.com
Open daily for dinner.

The bold colors of Picasso-like Impressionist artwork immediately catch the eye. Special wine selections from the 56 Degree Bar whet the palate and nightly specials "tantalize the taste buds." Along with calamari and charcuterie, there is a small plate choice as an appetizer. The entrées include options of fish, meat, vegetarian, or poultry prepared with a special combination of flavors and attractively presented. Truffles should definitely be considered a splurge.

TWENTY at Charley Creek Inn

111 West Market Street
Wabash, IN 46992
(260) 563-0111
www.charleycreekinn.com
Open Monday-Friday for breakfast, lunch & dinner;
Saturday & Sunday for brunch & dinner.

Located in the heart of downtown Wabash, The Charley Creek Inn was born in 1920 and reborn in 2009 as an historic boutique hotel. Appropriate to the history and true to its name, the Twenty Restaurant celebrates the 1920s era. Wall posters serve as reminders about events and sites of the past. Sheet music and background music commemorate the Wabash-connected Hoagy Carmichael and Cole Porter. Omelets are the most popular choices for breakfast. Lunch offers a lobster macaroni and cheese, pastas, sandwiches, and a variety of salads. In addition to butcher block steaks, the dinner menu includes fish, chicken, pork and pasta. Twenty also features a piano bar called the Green Hat Lounge with live weekend entertainment.

TWENTY TAP

5406-08 North College Avenue
Indianapolis, IN 46220
(317) 602-8840
www.twentytap.com
Open Monday for dinner; Tuesday-Sunday for lunch and dinner.

Obviously there were 20 taps when the doors first opened, but today there are 38. The bar has also grown in popularity and is a special neighborhood "go-to" restaurant. The food is a big step up from the normal bar fare. Seasoned fries with a choice of dipping sauces are clearly a trademark, as are the burgers with out-of-the-ordinary toppings. The salmon BLT is another good choice. Of course, there is a simple salad but also a more sophisticated moho pork cobb. The atmosphere is friendly and conversations among the tables are common.

TWIGS & SPRIGS TEAROOM

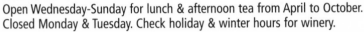

Stream Cliff Herb Farm & Winery
8225 South County Road 90 W
Commiskey, IN 47227
(812) 346-5859
www.streamclifffarm.com
Open Wednesday-Sunday for lunch & afternoon tea from April to October.
Closed Monday & Tuesday. Check holiday & winter hours for winery.

All of the Dining Secrets criteria is present here: out-of-the-way location, history, people and food. As you approach the town, look for a silo and greenhouse, then follow that to Stream Cliff Herb Farm. There is a 190-year history of the property and its development as Indiana's oldest herb farm. Today, there are multiple gardens depicting the pattern on a quilt, several old buildings, and a rustic tearoom sitting amongst the rows of flowers. The food incorporates the natural ingredients of the area, especially the herbs. For starters, there is a vegetable medley cheese soup. Follow it with a choice of dill and rosemary chicken salad, marjoram seafood salad, bird seed pasta salad, or a garden burger, turkey club or reuben sandwich. Dessert is a must with hummingbird cake at the top of the list. Afternoon country tea is served in keeping with the claim that "the taking of tea for a gardener is not a beverage, but a lifestyle." You can also enjoy a glass of wine in the tearoom from the on-site winery.

UKIYO

4907 North College Avenue
Indianapolis, IN 46205
(317) 384-1048
www.ukiyoindy.com
Open Tuesday-Sunday for lunch & dinner. Closed Monday.

Shaded windows, bubble walls and flowery paper lights make this Asian restaurant feel special. It is a great place to go to share tastes of small plates: sushi, sashimi, nigiri and maki rolls. The half or full orders of homemade ramen noodles are served in bowls of broth with a choice of veggies, fish or chicken. There is also a daily feature, Chirashi Donburi, which is a sushi rice bowl filled with fresh fish of the day, avocado, shiitake, konbu and horseradish. A special dining experience called Omakase can be arranged Tuesday-Saturday with seating at the sushi bar. The chef plans and prepares a surprise menu that even includes beverages.

UNION 50

620 North East Street
Indianapolis, IN 46202
(317) 610-0234
www.union-50.com
Open daily for dinner.

Just off Mass Ave., you must enter Union 50 from the walkway on the north side of the Trowel Trades Building. If you do, the floor-to-ceiling wall of bottles above the bar almost takes your breath away. The old space has been converted into a contemporary chic venue with high tables, regular tables, and long tables each inviting you to eat, drink and listen to live music. The menu is designed to be shared. You may select a charcuterie board with your choice of cheeses and extras. There are also petite plates, different styles of handcut fries, sauces and poutines. Bistro-type food and more hearty meals like pork chops and schnitzel are also offered.

UPTOWN CAFÉ

102 East Kirkwood Avenue
Bloomington, IN 47408
(812) 339-0900
www.the-uptown.com
Open Monday-Saturday for breakfast, lunch & dinner;
Sunday for brunch.

Located just off the downtown square, this upscale café attracts a broad cross-section of people in this busy college town. The cuisine is described as "American food with attitude." Breakfast includes standard eggs the way you love them, and a few ways that might surprise you: potato cream cheese omelettes, chorizo and eggs, and huevos rancheros. Lunch and dinner are a gumbo of flavors: big steaks, fresh fish, New Orleans favorites, etouffees and barbecued shrimp. Beer, wine, and cocktails are available.

VERA MAE'S BISTRO

207-209 South Walnut Street
Muncie, IN 47305
(765) 747-4941
www.veramaes.com
Open Monday-Friday for lunch & dinner; Saturday for dinner.
Closed Sunday.

As you enter this storefront restaurant, you know you are some place special. The atmosphere is inviting and the decor has a similar warmth with seasonal ornaments hanging from tree branches. Relax in the full lounge or at the bar that originally served patrons at grandmother Vera's diner. Enjoy piano music and jazz on Friday and Saturday evenings. A wide variety of lunch choices include Vera Mae's Cajun crab cake sandwich. If you are interested in hors d'oeuvres before dinner, try the baked brie or apple bacon cheddar fritters. Dinner entrées are equally imaginative with dill crusted cod and chicken brie raspberry among the selections. Of course, you must save room for the homemade desserts.

VIDA

601 East New York Street
Indianapolis, IN 46202
(317) 420-2323
www.vida-restaurant.com
Open Tuesday-Saturday for dinner. Closed Sunday & Monday.

Located in the heart of downtown Indianapolis, Vida has received recognition for its innovative dishes, unique space, and professional staff. Vida boasts Indy's only in-house hydroponic wall of greens. There is an ala carte menu and a "Chef's Tasting" menu, which is a five course meal paired with selected wines. For both dining styles, the chefs design the two menus around the seasons, using fresh local ingredients. The staff is well-versed in offering wine pairing tips for each dish.

VIET BISTRO

5763 East 86th Street
Indianapolis, IN 46250
(317) 598-1899
Open daily for lunch & dinner.

Located behind Castleton Square Mall, the Viet Bistro is an excellent escape from the busy activity of the area. The restaurant is carefully and comfortably appointed. The menu is not complicated and the staff are helpful. Appetizers include several kinds of spring rolls, salad and soup. Then, egg or rice noodles, tofu and stir fry or fried rice are offered with vegetables, chicken, pork or beef. For dessert, a banana fritter with coconut milk adds the perfect taste to a wonderful meal.

VITO PROVOLONE'S
8031 South Meridian Street
Indianapolis, IN 46217
(317) 888-1112
www.vitoprovolones.com
Open daily for dinner.

A red-headed Italian owns this restaurant, named after his grandfather Vito who is pictured in various places throughout the dining areas. Wine bottles filled with flowers decorate the tables; wine bottles filled with wine decorate the shelves. Dine in this casual atmosphere offering gourmet pizzas with names abbreviating the ingredients, such as S.M.O.G. (sausage, mushroom, onions, green peppers) and B.O.T. (bacon, onion, tomatoes). You can build your own pasta dish or enjoy chicken, beef or seafood prepared in a special Italian way. The menu tells the guest that "the PASTA-bilities are endless!"

WAGNER'S RIBS
361 Wagner Road
Porter, IN 46304
(219) 926-7614
Open daily for lunch & dinner.

After a long day at the dunes, stop by Wagner's for ribs: baby back, spare or country-style. They bottle their own tasty sauce and you can purchase some to take home. Sides of waffle fries, onion rings, coleslaw and cornbread cakes are choices to go with the entrées which, in addition to the ribs, include steak, chicken, pork, pollack and perch. If you prefer a sandwich, choose from Italian dip, hamburgers, or a fish 'n chips combo. Eli's cheesecakes are a delightful way to top off your meal. Wagner's has beer signs on the walls, labels on the tables, and serves many of the advertised beers. You must be 21 to enter this country bar.

WHISKY'S
334 Front Street
Lawrenceburg, IN 47025
(812) 537-4239
www.whiskysrestaurant.com
Open Monday-Friday for lunch & dinner; Saturday for dinner. Closed Sunday.

Old Lawrenceburg is the home of Seagram's Distillery, and the restaurant is named for its location in the "Whisky City." Two buildings, one dating from 1850 and the other rumored to have been a button factory in 1835, are joined by an atrium and feature five dining areas: a formal dining room, enclosed courtyard, Malt Room, Seagram's Room, and the cozy backroom bar. The overall atmosphere is dark and quiet with candles and fresh flowers on the tables. The atrium is decorated with a collection of birdhouses, and a post office from an old grocery store provides unique seating for four. Most in demand are the barbecued ribs smoked with a secret sauce, but the steaks and house-smoked chicken are other popular selections.

WHISTLE STOP RESTAURANT

10021 North U.S. Highway 421
Monon, IN 47959
(219) 253-4101
www.mononconnection.com
Open Tuesday-Sunday for lunch & dinner;
Saturday for breakfast. Closed Monday.

Enjoy a meal at the Whistle Stop before or after your visit to the adjacent museum. The menu offers soups, salads and sandwiches, along with dinner entrées carrying names like Train Wreck and Railroad Ties. Railroad history buffs will appreciate the museum's collection of artifacts and memorabilia from the past. Hundreds of old lanterns, authentic dining car china and silver, and restored brass locomotive bells and whistles are on display. There is also a full-size replica of the Illinois Central Depot. Eat at the Whistle Stop and receive a discount at the museum.

WILLARD

99 North Main Street
Franklin, IN 46131
(317) 738-9991
www.thewillard.com
Open daily for lunch & dinner.

The original brick home built on this site in 1860 is the core of the present structure. Eliza Willard and her niece and nephew, the Judahs, constructed a hotel around the home in 1922. Interestingly, Mrs. Willard and Mrs. Judah were active in the Prohibition Movement, and today the space is occupied by a pub and eatery. When the property was refurbished, care was taken to maintain the antique fixtures, the curved wooden staircase and the marble fireplace. The specialty is pizza, made by hand, but there is an extensive list of appetizers, sandwiches and salads. Mexican dishes, steak, chicken and seafood entrées are also on the menu. The Willard is touted as a place "where friends meet" for a drink and a bite to eat, and the outdoor seating area is a popular place to gather in nice weather.

WILLIE & RED'S

On State Road 38
Hagerstown, IN 47346
(765) 489-4131
www.willieandreds.com
Open Wednesday & Sunday for lunch; Thursday-Sunday for dinner.
Closed Monday & Tuesday.

Willie & Red's is a good place to have dinner after spending the day at the antique shops and mall nearby. It is a big place with a huge smorgasbord, but ordering off the menu is also available. While the restaurant generally looks much different than it did as Welliver's, the old bar is still comfortable and inviting. The cinnamon buns and the steaks continue to be recommended by diners.

WILLOW LEAVES OF HOPE

325 Jackson Street
Hope, IN 47246
(812) 546-0640
Open Monday, Tuesday, Thursday & Friday for lunch.
First and third Saturday each month for lunch.

Willow Leaves is a unique venue where lunch can be eaten amidst cleverly displayed antiques that are for sale. In addition to the normal lunch sandwiches and salads, there are daily specials and yummy desserts. Dinner theater productions are scheduled throughout the year with live music on the third Saturday evening of each month. Fried chicken and fish dinners are served on those nights. It is best to call for the schedule. When you visit, don't forget to check out the antiques.

WILSON-VAUGHAN HOSTESS HOUSE

723 West Fourth Street
Marion, IN 46953
(765) 664-3755
www.hostesshouse.org
Open Monday-Friday for lunch;
evenings & weekends for private parties only.

Built in 1912 by a wealthy Marion banker as a wedding gift to his bride, this historic mansion was the site of many parties, dinners and afternoon teas. Unfortunately, it was abandoned and vandalized in the 1940s, but a group of community-minded women refurbished the home and it now offers the Marion area a place for entertaining. Open to the public for lunch, visitors can dine on the sun porch, in the elegant dining room, or in other rooms of the beautifully appointed home. The menu includes a variety of sandwiches, salads, and extraordinary desserts.

WOODY'S LIBRARY RESTAURANT

40 East Main Street
Carmel, IN 46032
(317) 573-4444
www.woodyscarmel.com
Open daily for lunch & dinner.

This brick and limestone building was one of 164 libraries built in Indiana in the early 1900s as a gift from steel and railroad tycoon Andrew Carnegie. The interior has been transformed into an upscale restaurant; however, the shelves, books and antiques that are part of the decor preserve the intimate and inviting atmosphere of a small library. Beef, poultry, veal, pork and seafood entrées are embellished with wonderful sauces and glazes. The lunch menu offers several different sandwiches, salads and wraps. Woody's Place in the basement is a great spot for more casual dining or to wait for your table upstairs.

WORKINGMAN'S FRIEND

234 North Belmont Avenue
Indianapolis, IN 46222
(317) 636-2067
www.workingmansfriendindianapolis.com
Open Monday-Thursday & Saturday for lunch; Friday for lunch & dinner.
Closed Sunday.
CASH ONLY

It's not often that a person can go to an Indianapolis restaurant that has been around for a hundred years. Yes, three generations of the same family have been operating this establishment since 1918. During a period of hard times, the owner befriended his customers, letting them eat now and pay later, thus the name "Workingman's Friend." Today, one pays cash, no credit cards, for an excellent hamburger, tenderloin or braunschweiger sandwich, bean soup or homemade chili. They are famous for the double cheeseburger. Choices are made from a menu board posted over the bar.

YATS

5303 North College
Indianapolis, IN 46220
(317) 253-8817
www.yatscajuncreole.com
Open daily for lunch & dinner.

Joe claims that his place is for "Yats," people who love good food. "A Yat keeps livin' to eat." Order at the counter in this no frills restaurant. Samples are offered if you aren't sure what you want. The menu is Cajun, the flavors are spicy, and the number of choices is manageable. There are always vegetarian options along with gumbo, jambalaya, pazole stew, red beans, sausage and rice. All dishes are the same price; however, if you can't decide what you would like, you may order half of one entrée and half of another for an extra charge. The menu may change, but tasting is always an option.

ZAHARAKOS

329 Washington Street
Columbus, IN 47201
(812) 378-1900
www.zaharakos.com
Open daily for late breakfast, lunch & dinner.

Located in the same spot since 1900, Zaharakos has been completely renovated and the result is amazing. The original stained glass, carved oak woodwork and trim, marble soda fountains, and even the 1870s Welte orchestrion have all been restored to their natural beauty. Step inside the ice cream parlor and treat yourself to an old-fashioned ice cream soda, float, malt, or sundae with your choice of toppings and sauces. Breakfast is simply sandwiches, muffins and cinnamon rolls baked fresh daily. A variety of soups, salads and sandwiches are choices during the lunch and dinner hours. Visit the museum to see rare items from the 1800s, including antique syrup dispensers and the largest collection of pre-1900 marble soda fountains on public display.

ZODIAC

113 North Main Street
Crown Point, IN 46307
(219) 663-0303
www.zodiaccafelounge.com
Open Tuesday-Saturday for lunch & dinner. Closed Sunday & Monday.

The Zodiac invites you "to see what happens when the lights go down." There are several options for comfortable seating in this eclectic restaurant, including sitting outside. Daily specials are offered in the bar where you can enjoy entertainment provided by local singers and songwriters. The food shows a lot of variety and creativity with many items prepared on site. Sandwiches carry Greek names, the minotavros being a stuffed hamburger on a homemade pretzel bun. Salad ingredients include items such as sun-dried cranberries, smoked turkey and spinach. You don't have to wait until the sun sets to visit. It would be a good place to stop for lunch when en route to Chicago.

ZWANZIGZ PIZZA

1038 Lafayette Avenue
Columbus, IN 47201
(812) 376-0200
www.zwanzigzpizza.com
Open daily for lunch & dinner.

The owner, a former engineer, has put together a fine-tuned pizzeria. No wonder people claim that ZwanzigZ has the best pizza anywhere: fresh dough, spices, the best cheeses, and a few "secret" ZwanzigZ ingredients go into each made-to-order pizza. Salads, calzones and hoagies are offered as alternatives to the build your own or specialty pies. Beer and wine are available.

ZYDECO

11 East Main Street
Mooresville, IN 46158
(317) 834-3900
www.zydecos.net
Open Wednesday-Saturday for dinner. Closed Sunday-Tuesday.

The owners wanted to bring the tastes of South Louisiana to Central Indiana and they have done that and lots more. It is Mardi Gras every day at Zydeco and you will immediately get caught up in the celebration. There are streamers, twinkling lights, beads, jesters, and bold colors everywhere. The most exciting menu items are Cajun. A hearty choice of appetizers includes Crescent City boiled shrimp, oysters, tasso (highly seasoned smoked pork), and frog legs. Salads and soups–gumbo ya-ya, jambalaya, red beans and rice–are popular choices, along with Cajun entrées smothered in a thick, flavorful sauce termed "etouffee." The menu changes seasonally, and spring is the time for the crawfish boil. Specialty drinks are also available.

Tour Indiana
Monuments, Museums, Activities & More

ATLANTA

Mr. Muffin's Trains
165 East Main Street
Atlanta, IN 46031
(765) 292-2022

Located in an old flour mill, Mr. Muffin's Trains offers one of the largest model train collections, an "O Gauge" layout, and assistance for model train upkeep. Go on Saturday to see the trains running on the tracks.

AUBURN

Auburn Cord Duesenberg Automobile Museum
1600 South Wayne Street
Auburn, IN 46706
(260) 925-1444

Listed in the National Registry of Historic Places, this 80,000 square-foot building houses over 100 fascinating antique and classic cars from the early 1900s.

Kruse Museums
5634 County Road 11 A
Auburn, IN 46706
(260) 927-9144

This stop includes multiple museums for a few specific interests: the National Military History Center, Kruse Automotive & Carriage Museum, and the Baseball Museum. From specialty car exhibits and baseball memorabilia to military education, there's plenty to see and learn!

BATTLE GROUND

Farm at Prophetstown
3534 Prophetstown Road
Battle Ground, IN 47920
(765) 567-4700

The Farm is located in the Prophetstown State Park which offers hiking trails and campsites in the tall grass prairies of Indiana. View sustainable small scale farming on this 125 acre site. Learn about agriculture and horse-powered farming. Meat, eggs and other items are on sale in the gift shop. In addition, there is a rich history to learn about the early Native Americans who lived in Prophetstown.

Wolf Park
4004 East 800 North
Battle Ground, IN 47920
(765) 567-2265

Visitors can see wolves at close range living in a large natural enclosure. Wolf Park is also home to foxes and a small herd of bison which are often included in the presentations.

BEDFORD

Bluespring Caverns
1459 Bluespring Caverns Road
Bedford, IN 47421
(812) 279-9471

Enjoy an hour-long boat ride through the caverns. Camp overnight in Canyon Hall, high above the hidden banks of Myst'ry River.

CHESTERTON

Indiana Dunes Environmental Learning Center
700 Howe Road
Chesterton, IN 46304
(219) 395-9555

With the Indiana Dunes National Lakeshore as its classroom, students of all ages can learn about the relationship between people and the environment. Visit the dunes while you are there.

Tour Indiana

CLARKSVILLE

Falls of the Ohio State Park
201 West Riverside Drive
Clarksville, IN 47129
(812) 280-9970

The 386-million-year-old fossil beds in the park are among the largest naturally exposed Devonian fossil beds (coral reefs) in the world.

COLUMBUS

Columbus Area Visitors Center
506 Fifth Street
Columbus, IN 47201
(812) 378-2622

The Columbus Area Visitors Center, a renovated home built in the early 1860s, is the starting point for a walking tour that showcases the city's fine architecture, public art, garden and landscaping.

Miller House & Garden
Tours arranged through Columbus Area Visitors Center
506 Fifth Street
Columbus, IN 47201
(812) 378-2622 or (800) 468-6564

The National Historic Landmark 1953 home of Irwin and Xenia Miller presents international Modernist aesthetic design. The open layout flat roof structure with stone and glass walls and bright patterned textile decorations is highly acclaimed. The geometric gardens were created to complement the home's architecture.

CORYDON

Corydon Capitol State Historic Site
202 E. Walnut Street
Corydon, IN 47112
(812) 738-4890

Tour the state's original capitol building, built from local limestone and wood. It was completed around 1816. The site also includes an informative visitors center.

Zimmerman Art Glass Co.
300 East Chestnut Street
Corydon, IN 47112
(812) 738-2206

This is a rare opportunity to see artists work in the time-honored method of individual glass sculpting. The skill has been passed down to more than three generations, and their beautiful products are for sale.

CRAWFORDSVILLE

General Lew Wallace Study & Museum
200 Wallace Avenue
Crawfordsville, IN 47933
(765) 362-5769

Listed on the National Register of Historic Places, the museum is located in the private study of Major General Lew Wallace, the author of Ben-Hur. Items on display include memorabilia from his life as an author, soldier, statesman, artist, violinist, and inventor.

DALEVILLE

Canoe Country
6660 S. County Rd. 900 W
Daleville, IN 47334
(765) 378-7358

Canoe, kayak, or tube down the White River in north central Indiana. Several trip duration options are available, ranging from 2 to 17 miles. Campsites are also available for overnight rental.

Tour Indiana

DANA

Ernie Pyle WWII Museum
120 West Briarwood Avenue
Dana, IN 47847
(765) 665-3633

Visit the birthplace of Indiana born historic WWII correspondent Ernie Pyle. He was killed near Okinawa at the age of 44. The museum has a collection of memorabilia related to Pyle's reporting and the War.

EVANSVILLE

Willard Library
21 First Avenue
Evansville, IN 47710
(812) 425-4309

Housed in a 120-year-old historic Victorian Gothic building, it is the oldest public library building in the state. Legend states it's a living, breathing haunted house.

FAIRMOUNT

James Dean Gallery
425 North Main Street
Fairmount, IN 46928
(765) 948-3326

James Dean spent his early years in Fairmount. The gallery houses much of the memorabilia from his short active life: his high school interests, his love of cars and motorcycles, and his movie career. Dean is also buried in a cemetery in Fairmount.

FAIR OAKS

Fair Oaks Farms
856 North 600 East
Fair Oaks, IN 47943
(877) 536-1194

Fair Oaks houses one of the largest working dairies in the country, plus a birthing farm, cheese factory, garden with seasonal produce, and outside play area. There is also an ice cream parlor, cafe and large family sit-down restaurant.

FERDINAND

Monastery of the Immaculate Conception
802 East 10th Street
Ferdinand, IN 47532
(812) 367-1411

Listed in the National Register of Historic Places, you can take a tour of the church, grounds, and architecturally magnificent monastery.

FISHERS

Conner Prairie
13400 Allisonville Road
Fishers, IN 46038
(317) 776-6000

Visit this 1,400-acre nationally acclaimed living history museum where costumed interpreters depict the life and times of early settlers in an 1836 village. The grounds include a visitors center, picnic area, restaurant, and gift shop. The new Treetop Outpost features a 4-story treehouse for exploring, building and playing songs on outdoor instruments.

FORT WAYNE

Allen County Public Library Genealogy Center
900 Library Plaza
Fort Wayne, IN 46802
((260) 421-1225

Visit the largest public genealogy research library in America. Free services are offered for both the beginning and advanced researchers.

Tour Indiana

FOUNTAIN CITY

Levi and Catharine Coffin State Historic Site
201 U.S. 27 North
Fountain City, IN 47341
(765) 847-1691

A National Historic Landmark, the home of Levi and Catharine Coffin once served as a main stop on the Underground Railroad. As prominent members of the community, the Coffins helped hundreds of slaves with transportation, clothing, food, and shelter on their way to freedom. Tour the house, learn more about the Underground Railroad, and hear the stories of those the couple helped.

GOSHEN

Old Bag Factory
1100 North Chicago Avenue
Goshen, IN 46528
(574) 534-2502

This historic 80,000 square foot building, originally a bag factory, houses a gallery of specialty shops and artisan workshops. On the second floor, there is a space named OBF Historical Gallery, which is home to many of the tools and memorabilia from the old factory.

GREENFIELD

Tuttle Orchards
5717 North 300 West
Greenfield, IN 46140
(317) 326-2278

There is something for everyone to enjoy in a visit to Tuttle Orchards: the green house appeals to the gardener; the farm store and café offer fresh produce and prepared pies, jellies and fruits; there are plenty of activities for kids. Apples can be picked when the season is right.

HAGERSTOWN

Wilbur Wright Birthplace
1525 North 750 East
Hagerstown, IN 47346
(765) 332-2495

Visit the birthplace of one of the first pioneers of flight. You can tour the family home, visit a museum, and see a replica of the Wright Flyer. Step back in time with a stroll down Main Street and learn more about Kitty Hawk.

HOBART

Albanese Candy Factory & Store
5441 East U.S. 30
Hobart, IN 46410
(219) 947-3070

Tour the factory and see gummies and chocolates being made, along with the world's tallest chocolate waterfall—an experience that both children and adults won't soon forget! Samples are handed out for tasting and, of course, available for purchase in the outlet store.

HUNTINGTON

Dan Quayle Center/United States Vice Presidential Museum
815 Warren Street
Huntington, IN 46750
(260) 356-6356

The museum is in a renovated church and has two floors. The first floor features the history of U.S. Vice Presidents. The second floor houses memorabilia and a theater.

Tour Indiana

INDIANAPOLIS

Children's Museum of Indianapolis
3000 North Meridian Street
Indianapolis, IN 46208
(317) 334-4000

The largest children's museum in the world houses hands-on galleries exploring the physical and natural sciences, world cultures, sports and a collection of American memorabilia. Outside, there is the Sports Legends Experience that highlights outstanding Indiana athletes and invites participation in basketball, football, baseball, golf, hockey, track, tennis, climbing, and auto racing.

Crown Hill Cemetery
700 West 38th Street
Indianapolis, IN 46208
(317) 925-3800

One of the most historically significant sites in Indiana, Crown Hill is the burial site of many of Indiana's most famous people and public servants. The beautiful grounds include a large population of wildlife and over 150 species of trees and plant life.

The Eiteljorg Museum
500 West Washington Street
Indianapolis, IN 46204
(317) 636-WEST (9378)

The only museum of its kind in the Midwest, it contains one of the best Native American and Western art collections in the world.

Fort Harrison State Park
6000 N. Post Road
Indianapolis, IN 46216
(317) 591-0904

The park includes one of the largest tracts of hardwood forest in Central Indiana. Activities available include: cultural arts programs, a nature center, fishing, hiking and biking trails, saddle barn with horses, and the famous Fort Harrison Golf Course.

Indiana Medical History Museum
3045 West Vermont Street
Indianapolis, IN 46222
(317) 635-7329

Tour the exhibits in the Old Pathology Building on the grounds of the former Central State Hospital and learn about the beginnings of psychiatry and medical developments.

Indianapolis Motor Speedway Museum
4790 West 16th Street
Indianapolis, IN 46222
(317) 492-8500

Learn about the history of auto racing and view approximately 75 vehicles on display at all times. Bus tours of the historic 2.5-mile oval are available.

Indiana State Capitol
200 West Washington Street
Indianapolis, IN 46204
(317) 233-5293

The building is home to the state of Indiana's legislative, judicial and executive branches of government. The House and Senate chambers can be viewed, as well as statues and artifacts from Indiana's history. Tours are available.

Indiana State Museum
650 West Washington Street
Indianapolis, IN 46204
(317) 232-1637

With over 40,000 square feet of exhibit space and over 300,000 artifacts in collections, the museum covers the history of the natural world, Native Americans, culture, and the future of Indiana.

Tour Indiana

International Marketplace
3685 Commercial Drive
Indianapolis, IN 46222
(317) 550-1600

The International Marketplace is a west side neighborhood where the many cultures of the Indianapolis community come to eat, shop and enjoy. 38th Street is the major access road. An "information desk" is located at this Commercial Drive address where there is a museum with artifacts donated by the ethnic groups of the city. Get ideas on what stores to visit and foods to try from Ethiopia, Vietnam, Africa, Japan, China, Pakistan, Mexico and more. All of these options are within a few streets of each other. You can also learn about dining tours and cultural activities.

Madame Walker Theatre Center
617 Indiana Avenue
Indianapolis, IN 46202
(317) 236-2099

Located in the restored 1920 headquarters of Madame C.J. Walker, the first self-made African-American female millionaire in the country. The Center is dedicated to celebrating arts and culture from an African-American perspective, along with events directed toward cross-cultural appreciation.

Newfields
(Indianapolis Museum of Art)
4000 Michigan Road
Indianapolis, IN 46208
(317) 920-2651

The museum boasts a permanent historical collection of more than 50,000 works of art. Tour the Virginia B. Fairbanks Art and Nature Park and Oldfields-Lilly House and Gardens.

KENDALLVILLE
Mid-America Windmill Museum
732 South Allen Chapel Road
Kendallville, IN 46755
(260) 347-2334

Learn about the evolution of wind power in the only known operational museum of its kind in the United States.

KNIGHTSTOWN
Hoosier Gymnasium
355 North Washington Street
Knightstown, IN 46148
(765) 345-2100

This famous gym was home to the Hickory Huskers in the movie "Hoosiers." Shoot a basket from where Jimmy made the game-winning shot or just sit in the stands and relive one of the greatest sports movies of all time. Call for times.

LINCOLN CITY
Lincoln Boyhood National Memorial
3027 East South Street
Lincoln City, IN 47552
(812) 937-4541

The first national park established in Indiana, it preserves the site of the farm where Abraham Lincoln lived during his formative years.

LOGANSPORT
Cass County Dentzel Carousel
Riverside Park
1208 Riverside Drive
Logansport, IN 46947
(574) 753-8725

Listed as a National Historic Landmark, this beautifully restored merry-go-round is a masterpiece of carving by Gustav Dentzel, dating back to 1902. For a $1.00 a ride, you can reach for the golden ring from one of over 40 hand-carved animals and chariots. Seasonal hours.

Tour Indiana

MARENGO

Marengo Cave
400 East State Road 64
Marengo, IN 47140
(888) 702-2837 or (812) 365-2705

Take a leisurely tour through the Crystal Palace, pan for gemstones, twist and crawl through the cave simulator, or explore an undeveloped natural cave in this U.S. National landmark.

MONTGOMERY

Gasthof Amish Village
6659 East Gasthof Village Road
One Mile North of US 50
Montgomery, IN 47558
(812) 486-4900

A barn constructed by Amish carpenters houses a restaurant buffet loaded with homemade lunch and dinner items. The adjacent bakery has breads, jams, pies, and cakes you can take home. Gift items are offered in the three stores in the village. Seasonal flea markets also take place. The Village is on 92 acres and there is an inn if you want to spend the night.

NASHVILLE

Melchior Marionette Theatre
76 South Van Buren Street
Nashville, IN 47448
(800) 849-4853

This unique outdoor venue offers 20-minute family-oriented cabaret variety shows featuring handcrafted marionettes. Open May, June, July, September and October. For the schedule of performances, workshops and camps during other months, contact Peewinkle's Puppet Studio at www.peewinklespuppets.com.

T.C. Steele's State Historic Site
4220 T.C. Steele Road
Nashville, IN 47448
(812) 988-2785

Guided tours of the House of the Singing Winds, the studio where changing exhibits display Steele's work, are scheduled regularly. You can also visit the Dewar Log Cabin and the 90 acre Selma Steele Nature Preserve.

NEW CASTLE

Indiana Basketball Hall of Fame
One Hall of Fame Court
New Castle, IN 47362
(765) 529-1891

Located near the world's largest high school gym, the museum features displays, exhibits, artifacts, and memorabilia depicting Indiana high school basketball history. Visit the locker room for John Wooden's "pep talk."

NEW HARMONY

Historic New Harmony
401 North Arthur Street
New Harmony, IN 47631
(800) 231-2168

One of the most significant utopian communities in America, this is a place where three centuries of architecture, history and innovation interact. Buildings from the early and mid-19th century are within the district, including a museum, library, gallery and opera house. There are dining and shopping opportunities, along with historic guest houses and small bed & breakfasts for overnight accommodations.

Tour Indiana

PAOLI

Wilstem
4229 US-150 West
Paoli, IN 47454
(812) 936-4484

Sitting on more than 1,000 acres in southern Indiana, Wilstem offers cabin lodging, zipline tours, horseback riding, and animal encounters with elephants, kangaroos, giraffes and more. Reservations for animal encounters and activities are encouraged.

PERU

Circus Hall of Fame
3076 East Circus Lane
Peru, IN 46970
(765) 472-7553

The museum's collection includes vintage circus wagons, steam calliopes, costumes of famous performers, circus props and other artifacts, posters, and handbills from circuses around the world.

Grissom Air Museum
1000 West Hoosier Boulevard
Peru, IN 46970
(765) 689-8011

One of the nation's fastest growing aviation museums, you can learn about historic aircraft, climb the observation tower, view exciting exhibits, and enjoy a modern, hands-on facility.

SOUTH BEND

South Bend Chocolate Factory
3300 West Sample Street
South Bend, IN 46619
(574) 233-2577

Take a factory tour where you can sample straight off the production line and view one of the world's largest collections of chocolate-related artifacts.

Studebaker National Museum
201 Chapin Street
South Bend, IN 46601
(574) 235-9714

Studebaker automobiles were manufactured in South Bend. The Museum has three floors and includes the world's largest collection of presidential carriages plus wagons, vintage cars, military vehicles, lots of car culture history and interactive exhibits.

TERRE HAUTE

CANDLES Holocaust Museum
1532 South 3rd Street
Terre Haute, IN 47802
(812) 234-7881

CANDLES (Children of Auschwitz Nazi Deadly Lab Experiments Survivors) is an organization founded by Eva Kor, who was a twin and therefore a subject for the Mengele research. This is the only organization and museum dedicated to the memory of the survivors of the twin experiments at Auschwitz.

Clabber Girl Museum & Country Store
900 Wabash Avenue
Terre Haute, IN 47807
(812) 232-9446

Tour this renovated museum, country store, and bake shop and learn about the history of Clabber Girl baking powder. Museum exhibits include examples of Hulman & Co. products and brands, an antique racecar from the Indianapolis Motor Speedway, and a Clabber Girl delivery wagon. Antique household items, kitchen appliances, vintage toys, and an old-fashioned coal generator are also on display.

Tour Indiana

VINCENNES

George Rogers Clark National Monument
401 South 2nd Street
Vincennes, IN 47591
(812) 882-1776

Named for the Revolutionary War commander, the memorial is considered a major feat in architectural engineering and is the largest National Park Service monument outside of Washington D.C. Picnic in the park or take the sidewalks to downtown Vincennes.

Grouseland, William Henry Harrison Mansion & Museum
3 West Scott Street
Vincennes, IN 47591
(812) 882-2096

In 1804, when Indiana was still a territory, then Governor William Henry Harrison built Grouseland. It was the first brick home in Indiana and is a National Historical Monument. Later, Harrison became the ninth U.S. President. The museum in the home has artifacts from early presidential campaigns and from the Battle of Tippecanoe.

Red Skelton Museum of American Comedy
20 West Red Skelton Boulevard
Vincennes University
Vincennes, IN 47591
(812) 888-4184

Learn about the life of one of America's great comedians with Hoosier roots. The Museum has colorful displays and the interactive activities are fun and engaging: a character gallery with costumes and a radio sound booth are two examples. Check out Red's Pledge of Allegiance presentation and the gallery of his original artwork. A performing arts center is attached to the Museum and offers theater presentations.

WINCHESTER

SilverTowne Coin Shop
120 East Union City Pike
Winchester, IN 47394
(877) 477-2646

One of America's largest and most respected rare coin dealers, you will find an incredible coin collection of all types and dates, along with quality precious metal gifts, hand-crafted original jewelry designs, and collectibles.

ZIONSVILLE

Traders Point Creamery
9101 Moore Road
Zionsville, IN 46077
(317) 733-1700

Both kids and adults will enjoy touring this dairy farm. Watch the cows being milked, see the calves in their pen, view the pre-Civil War barns, visit the farmers market, and don't miss the upstairs café and dairy bar.

The Village of Zionsville
135 South Elm Street
Zionsville, IN 46077
(317) 873-3836

One of a few towns in the United States that has preserved its brick main street, the village has more than 50 shops, from fashionable to rare and vintage antiques. Nestled among the shops are numerous restaurants and quaint cafés.

Sweets and Treats

ATLANTA
Lisa's Pie Shop
5995 South U.S. 31
Atlanta, IN 46031
(317) 758-6944
www.lisapies.com

Need a pie? Go to an award-winning bakery just north of Indianapolis on U.S. 31. The blue ribbons line the walls around counters and coolers filled with fruit and cream pies. Some days 500 pies are sold, and they're all made on site. Unsold pies are crumbled and put in jars for sale; scoop some out of the jar, heat it up and top it with ice cream!

BROOKSTON
Klein Brot Haus Bakery
106 East 3rd Street
Brookston, IN 47923
(765) 563-3788

Their pies can be found at farmer's markets in the central Indiana area. They are based in Brookston where you can also find a wide selection of cookies and breads straight from the oven. If it is breakfast or lunch time, there is the opportunity to sit down and grab a bite to eat before attacking the desserts.

FLOYDS KNOBS
Berry Twist Ice Cream
3660 Paoli Pike Suite, #3
Floyds Knobs, IN 47119
(812) 923-8305
www.berrytwist.com

Berry Twist has been a southern Indiana ice cream staple since 1978 and the traditions and neighborhood favorites continue. Known for their sherbet, they also offer the usual ice cream treats like cones, sundaes, frozen coffees, floats, and slushies.

FORTVILLE
Sunrise Bakery
101 West Broadway Street
Fortville, IN 46040
(317) 485-7574
www.sunrisebakeries.com

Choose from a selection of handmade donuts, local coffee, and smoothies. Make sure the kids keep an eye out for the live train set up inside.

GREENVILLE
Capriole Farms
10329 New Cut Road
Greenville, IN 47124
(812) 923-9408
www.capriolegoatcheese.com

Famous for their homemade cheese, a store located on the farm invites visitors to sample and purchase a wide variety of fresh, aged, and specialty cheeses.

HAGERSTOWN
Abbott's Candies
48 East Walnut Street
Hagerstown, IN 47346
(877) 801-1200
www.abbottscandy.com

The big pink and white building is a favorite stop for families who come to watch the candy-making process. The final stop on a tour is to see the chocolates being packed in their elegant gift boxes.

Sweets and Treats

INDIANAPOLIS

Best Chocolate in Town
880 Massachusetts Avenue
Indianapolis, IN 46204
(317) 636-2800

As soon as you open the door to this independent chocolate shop, smells of freshly made sweets waft over you. Cases full of truffles, sea-salt caramels, toffee, and more, fill the front of the store.Be sure to check out the locally-made ice cream and gelato.

Cake Bake Shop
6515 Carrollton Avenue
Indianapolis, IN 46220
(317) 257-2253
www.thecakebakeshop.com

Whimsical seasonal decorations and large cases filled with beautiful cakes and sweets greet you as you walk into this award-winning bakery and lunch spot. You will most likely need a reservation if you want to enjoy a meal, but you can always pick up a slice of cake; Oprah's favorite is the Mint Chocolate Chip. Don't miss the picture window for a peek at the baking process.

Delicias Jalisco
3851 Georgetown Road
Indianapolis, IN 46254
(317) 875-1555

If you fancy a yogurt smoothie, frozen fruit treats like chocolate-dipped bananas, a popsicle, or yummy ice cream, this colorful dessert spot is the right choice! The fresca con cream (strawberries whipped with yogurt) is especially delicious. It's a great place to get a sweet after dining at a restaurant in the International Marketplace.

Heidelberg Haus
7625 Pendleton Pike
Indianapolis, IN 46226
(317) 547-1230
www.heidelberghaus.com

Have you ever wondered what eating an award-winning pastry surrounded by 800 gnomes would be like? Heidelberg Haus on Indy's eastside has had the same location, menu, and owner for more than 45 years. Cozy and charming, it houses a café, gift shop, grocery and bakery. Enjoy your treats in the eclectic surroundings of nesting dolls, steins, and gnomes.

Just Pop In!
6406 Cornell Avenue
Indianapolis, IN 46220
(317) 257-9338
www.justpopinpopcorn.com

What started as a small popcorn shop has grown into a nationally-recognized yet locally invested popcorn powerhouse. The idea was created by twin sisters inspired by their nights popping corn with their grandfather. Both traditional and new flavor combinations are available, along with specialized treats for parties or events. Their fun, new space in Broad Ripple has popcorn, small plates, beer and wine.

Long's Bakery
1453 North Tremont Street
Indianapolis, IN 46222
(317) 632-3741

Don't let the line or cash only policy deter you; Long's donuts and baked goods are worth it. An Indianapolis staple since 1955, you'll meet people from all over the city who travel to have these scratch-baked doughnuts, cookies, and cakes. Take a peek in the back of the shop and see the signature yeast doughnuts being made.

Sweets and Treats

Rene's Bakery
6524 B N. Cornell Avenue
Indianapolis, IN 46220
(317) 251-2253
www.renesbakery.com

Nestled in the north end of Broad Ripple, Rene's Bakery is a village favorite. With a variety of handmade breads, croissants, cookies, tarts, and cakes, the small bakery has been delivering big flavors since 2004. Closed Mondays and Tuesdays, grab your sweet treats or place your special orders Wednesday-Sunday.

JEFFERSONVILLE
Schimpff's Confectionery, LLC
347 Spring Street
Jeffersonville, IN 47130
(812) 283-8367
www.schimpffs.com

Operating in its original location since 1891, Schimpff's is one of the longest-running family-owned candy businesses in the U.S. Red Hots are their oldest continuously made candy, but they are also known for candy fish and horehound drops. Watching the candy being made is a lot of fun. Antiques and treasures of the candy-making industry are on display.

KOKOMO
**J. Edwards Gourmet –
Fine Chocolates & Gourmet Cakes**
2106 West Sycamore Street
Kokomo, IN 46901
(765) 626-0142
www.jedwardsgourmet.com

Voted best dessert place in Kokomo, this north central Indiana chocolate shop offers more than 60 types of chocolate and more than 30 cake varieties. From pecan clusters and chocolate covered strawberries to black forest cake and mandarin orange cake, J. Edwards has a treat for every occasion.

LEBANON
Donaldson's Finer Chocolates
600 S.outh State Road 39
Lebanon, IN 46052
(765) 482-3334
www.donaldsonschocolates.com

Opened by the current owners in 1966, Donaldson's has gone through some name changes and expansions, but the dedication to quality chocolate has remained the same. Although in an unlikely location off of I-65, these chocolate-covered treats are perfect for those who want fine chocolate made the old-fashioned way.

MADISON
Horst's Bakery Haus Hilltop
220 Clifty Drive
Madison, IN 47250
(812) 265-1295

Horst, the baker behind the shop's name, came to the United States from Germany in 1973. He opened the bakery in 2004 and continues some traditions with German ice box cookies, pastries, and donuts. It's recommended to get there early if you want to pick your favorites, but you can also stop in for breakfast and enjoy the atmosphere.

MCCORDSVILLE
Tim's Bakery
6087 West Broadway
McCordsville, IN 46055
(317) 335-3344

The sign on the window says, "Fresh Donuts." And that means baked every day. One customer reported that when there were no more blueberry donuts, the friendly staff suggested a 15 minute wait while a new batch was prepared.

Sweets and Treats

NEW ALBANY
Rookie's Cookies
310 Pearl Street
New Albany, IN 47150
(812) 948-8858
www.rookiescookies.net

Imagine cookies so delicious that the recipes are controlled by the family who created them. Intrigued? Try Rookie's Cookies, a neighborhood bakery that has been around since 1939. In addition to the famous butter cookies, this bakery makes pastries, pies, bread, and cakes.

PENDLETON
Quack Daddy Donuts
106 West State Street
Pendleton, IN 46064
(765) 221- 9174

If you like donuts with some flair, like Oreo, bacon, Fruity Pebbles, or M&M's, this place is for you. Featuring a variety of donuts, icings and toppings, you can order your favorite combo or just stick to plain glaze. Thirsty? Try a coffee or their specialty drink – chocolate milk in a frosty glass.

ROCHESTER
Sallie's by the Shore
1773 East 9th Street
Rochester, IN 46975
(574) 242- 2712

Handcrafted ice cream by a lake? What a treat! Sallie's by the Shore is housed in a revamped mobile trailer with a charming vintage vibe and Lake Manitou in the background. They have a variety of flavors, including pumpkin spice or carrot cake. Come for the ice cream, stay for the outdoor atmosphere.

TOPEKA
Yoder Popcorn Shoppe
7680 West 200 South
Topeka, IN 46571
(260) 768-4051
www.yoderpopcorn.com

The Yoder family first shared their popcorn with neighbors back in 1936. Now, the Shoppe offers a variety of kernels, oils, seasonings, gift baskets, and popcorn poppers. Visit them in Shipshewana's Amish country.

UPLAND
Ivanhoe's
979 South Main Street
Upland, IN 46989
(765) 998-7261
www.ivanhoes.info

If you have a craving for delicious ice cream, you must stop at Ivanhoe's, but you'll have to choose from more than 100 different selections. Ivanhoe's started as a drive-in in the '60s and has grown into a large, popular place to eat. In addition to ice cream treats, good old-fashioned hamburgers and excellent salads are just another reason to stop here.

WINCHESTER
Mrs. Wick's Bakery & Cafe
100 Cherry Street
Winchester, IN 47394
(765) 584-7437
www.wickspies.com

Wick's Pies opened this bakery & cafe in 1986, serving breakfast all day, but there are lunch and dinner options too. Dessert is decision-making time with so many choices for a slice of pie. An outlet store is located in the cafe and pies of all kinds are available to take home. The Wick's Pie Plant is nearby and tours are offered; call ahead to make arrangements.

Alphabetical Index of Restaurants

Alphabetical Index of Restaurants
(Continued)